DISPATCHES
FROM
MORMON
ZION

DISPATCHES FROM MORMON ZION

Ryan W. Davis

WILLIAM B. EERDMANS PUBLISHING COMPANY
GRAND RAPIDS, MICHIGAN

Wm. B. Eerdmans Publishing Co.
2006 44th Street SE, Grand Rapids, MI 49508
www.eerdmans.com

Published 2025

Book design by Leah Luyk

Printed in the United States of America

31 30 29 28 27 26 25   1 2 3 4 5 6 7

ISBN 978-0-8028-8469-5

Library of Congress Cataloging-in-Publication Data

A catalog record for this book is available from the Library of Congress.

Contents

Contents

Foreword

Observers have characterized Mormonism[1] as everything from "The American Religion" (Harold Bloom) to the "Great Modern Abomination" (too numerous to list). Whether Mormonism is a robust expression of Christianity or outside of it entirely is a theological question—and not this book's concern.

A less controversial question has to do with the status of Mormonism itself as a particular kind of community that seems to have sociologists flummoxed. Some have labeled the Mormon people "a subculture";[2] others call it an "indigenously developed ethnic minority" or "an incipient nationality."[3] Joel Kotkin pre-

1. The preferred designation for the church is The Church of Jesus Christ of Latter-day Saints. "Mormon" is a broader and less doctrinally circumscribed term for the cultural entity associated with the faith.

2. Armand Mauss's reference to Mormonism as a "subculture" appears to be common practice among sociologists. See his "Sociological Perspectives on the Mormon Subculture," *Annual Review of Sociology* 10 (1984): 437–60. Jan Shipps, Mauss indicates, "has also revealed a tendency to continue thinking of even contemporary Mormons in ethnic terms." See Armand Mauss, *The Angel and the Beehive: The Mormon Struggle with Assimilation* (Urbana: University of Illinois Press, 1994), 64–66 and 74n.

3. Dean L. May is paraphrasing Thomas O'Dea's claim. May, "Mormons," in *Harvard Encyclopedia of American Ethnic Groups*, ed. Stephan Thernstrom, Ann Orlov, and Oscar Handlin (Cambridge, MA: Harvard University Press, 1980), 720. As early as 1954, O'Dea refers to the Mormons as a "near nation," an "incipient nationality," a "subculture with its own peculiar conceptions and values," and "a people." See Thomas O'Dea, "Mormonism

ferred the term "a global tribe,"[4] and Bloom called the Latter-day Saints "a religion that became a people."[5] Clearly, a remarkable blend of shared history, theological peculiarity, communitarian ethic, and high-demand discipleship have forged bonds that far transcend simple denominational status.

I have attended Latter-day Saint worship services in places as far-flung as Ghana, Singapore, Brazil, and Kosovo. And like millions of my coreligionists, I have experienced the immediate intimacy, trust, and kinship that is a commonplace of what it means to be a Mormon. Saints use the term *Zion* as a fill in for this community, which is more an aspirational designation than something that is fully realized. In Mormonspeak, *Zion* can refer to the intensely distilled form that Mormonism takes in Utah country—the heart of the Mormon culture region. When Saints employ the term *Zion* in this way, it is often with a gently wry smile. For the Saints recognize in that word all the connotations understood by family members in response to a familiar story tinged equally with affection and humor.

How to convey the essence of that story to one outside the faith? Explorer Richard Burton may have been the most successful European ever to blend into the Arab cultures he studied in the nineteenth century, but even he sensed that "there is in Mormondom . . . an inner life into which I cannot flatter myself or deceive the reader with the idea of my having penetrated."[6]

---

and the Avoidance of Sectarian Stagnation: A Study of Church, Sect, and Incipient Nationality," *American Journal of Sociology* 60, no. 3 (November 1954): 285–93.

4. Joel Kotkin, *Tribes: How Race, Religion and Identity Determine Success in the New Global Economy* (New York: Random House, 1993), 245–49.

5. Harold Bloom, *The American Religion* (New York: Chu Hartley Publishers, 2006).

6. Richard Burton, *City of the Saints: Among the Mormons and Across the Rocky Mountains to California*, ed. Fawn M. Brodie (New York: Knopf, 1963), 224.

Stories, then, might be the best way to begin. And few writers tell a story better than Ryan Davis. They are stories of pheasant hunting, pie-baking contests, a riddling God, and the legend of one Quint McCallister.

Reading these essays feels like an evening around a campfire with the murmur of conversation—and the more one pays attention to the conversation the more interesting it gets. By the end, as with all good campfires, all of us will know ourselves and each other a little more generously.

Terryl Givens

Preface

"Well, I guess I'm heading out," Dave said. The party was winding down, though a few people lingered at this midwinter weeknight hot chocolate gathering of Boston-area Latter-day Saints. For the preceding two years of grad school, Dave and I had been roommates—along with three other members of our faith—in a small East Cambridge apartment.

I held up my hand from across the room. "See you back at the ranch," I said.

"I'll see you in Zion," Dave replied.

The line was the first of a call-and-response. In my childhood home, church films were the only allowable television on Sunday mornings. The most famous of these was *Legacy*, the story of "a Mormon journey" into the West.[1] By saying it was famous, I mean that almost everyone who grew up in the church knew the movie well, and no one outside the church had ever heard of it. My sister had watched it every Sunday morning for months. It's part love story, part drama. In the film's most iconic scene, Eliza is leaving for the West while her husband is joining up with the Mormon Battalion. A standard gimmick around our

1. *Legacy: A Mormon Journey*, directed by Kieth Merrill (Salt Lake City, UT: The Church of Jesus Christ of Latter-day Saints, 1993), 53 minutes.

apartment was to quote the characters' parting lines whenever anyone was going anywhere, however trivial.

"If I ever see you again," I said, allowing the prescribed dramatic pause, "it'll be Zion to me."

The exchange proceeded exactly as it usually did. This time, however, Megan—sitting on the couch nearby—overheard. She looked up from her conversation as if uncertain what just happened.

"That was . . ." she started, as if finding her way to her own reaction, "*surprisingly beautiful.*" Megan had not seen the movie, but she did have the concept of Zion. Or, more particularly, she had the distinctively Mormon concept of Zion.

◆ ◆ ◆

Latter-day Saints' scriptures define Zion as the "pure in heart." Zion is a people who are "of one heart and one mind, and [dwell] in righteousness." Among the Latter-day Saints, the aspiration for Zion started as a desire to build a physical city, first in Missouri and finally in the Salt Lake Basin. It was attended by an expansive economic program, which aimed to fulfill another of Zion's theological criteria: that "there were no poor among them." Expelled from Missouri and later from Illinois, the Saints imagined their westward journey as their own exodus to a promised land. There, they imagined fulfilling Deutero-Isaiah's prophecy calling all nations to Zion.[2]

I'll start with two apologies. First, I don't mean to suggest that the Latter-day Saints were unusual in their ambitions. Their aspiration was ordinary in its historical moment. The

---

2. Joel Kaminsky and Anne Stewart, "God of All the World: Universalism and Developing Monotheism in Isaiah 40–66," *Harvard Theological Review* 99, no. 2 (April 2006): 139–63, https://tinyurl.com/3u9ea3c4.

language of Zion permeated nineteenth-century American religious fervor.³ Second, I should acknowledge up front that the
ambition to build a Zion community could sometimes lead to
moral disaster.⁴

This book is not about the history of the concept or its reception in the early Church of Jesus Christ of Latter-day Saints.
Instead, I'm interested in its contemporary resonance. My own
memory extends to a time when members of the church in Utah
would contrast "Zion" with "the world" or, alternatively, "the
mission field." That language has now faded from use, and I
don't aim to revive it. What has remained is the Zion concept,
or anyway a specific redeployment of that concept, which I'm
going to call Mormon Zion.

I'm not totally sure I can get away with this. In the past, at-
tempts to stretch the Zion concept have not always fared well.
Awed by the natural beauty they encountered on the North Fork
of the Virgin River in Utah, an expedition of settlers named the
canyon Zion.⁵ Isaac Behunin, who had been in the church since
its New York origins, hoped that there he would finally find the
long-promised divine refuge. When Brigham Young visited the
settlement in 1870, he objected to the name on the grounds that
"it is not Zion." Thereafter, the settlers gamely called their valley "Not Zion," though today the original has won out as the
official name of the canyon's famous national park.

More recently, the Latter-day Saints have distanced themselves from the name Mormon. This is understandable. Though

3. Eran Shalev, *American Zion: The Old Testament as a Political Text from
the Revolution to the Civil War* (New Haven, CT: Yale University Press, 2014).

4. Matthew W. Dougherty, *Lost Tribes Found: Israelite Indians and Religious Nationalism in Early America* (Norman: University of Oklahoma Press,
2021).

5. "Zion: LDS Roots Are Part of Park History," Church News, May 16,
1992, https://tinyurl.com/mt4hwuse.

he adopted the name, Joseph Smith noted that Mormon was a label given to the movement by its enemies. With due apologies, I propose to retain the term "Mormon Zion." Most of the essays here are about living in Utah County, the place with the highest concentration of Latter-day Saints in the world. But I don't have in mind Utah in particular. My family is from Idaho, and I grew up in rural Arizona—not far from Snowflake, a desert grassland named not for the weather but because it was the place where Elder Snow and Elder Flake together founded a settlement. There is no exact geographical term for the cultural experience I want to explore, in part because it is not demarcated by any political boundary. Nor do I have in mind the formal institution of the church. Rather, the essays here are mostly about aspects of the culture that travel in company with church membership, though neither a formal part of it nor limited to it. I'm interested in the idioms, game nights, names, celebrations, foods, relationships, and so on that outsiders might recognize as "Mormon"—or, in some cases, might not recognize at all. I will call it Mormon Zion, but like the settlers mentioned above, I'd be happy to retreat to calling it *Not* Mormon Zion if others protest.

◆　◆　◆

Have you encountered another person—maybe someone you've never met—and for some reason, you can just tell what kind of experience they're having? Maybe you've caught a stranger's glance across a room and realized they were reacting to what was happening in that moment in just the same way you were. Maybe you were standing in a line, and the couple in front of you exchange a joke, and you happen to laugh, and they happily include you. Maybe they even take some special delight in the fact that you *also* got it. There can be a million small situations like this. What's distinctive about them is that they produce a sense of intimacy that doesn't depend on any prior shared experiences. Instead, there's just something about that other person that gives you the sense that the two of you somehow can see eye to eye. You are separate persons but share a feeling.

I'm not sure if this has anything to do with what Persian-period Judeans would have felt as they journeyed back to their former homeland, heeding prophetic calls to return to Zion. I'm also not sure it would make any sense to early nineteenth-century American Christians (among them the Latter-day Saints) intent on building a Zion in America. I'm not even sure if this is the feeling other contemporary members of the faith are talking about when they think of the Latter-day Saint scriptural verses about being "of one heart and one mind." But it is one way of understanding how sharing another person's cognitive and affective states can be meaningful to both people. And this feeling is what I mean by Mormon Zion.

The essays in this book are trying to get at a cluster of questions: What is Mormon Zion like? What kind of experiences does it make possible? If you encounter another person in the way where you *just get* what's happening to them, and they somehow intuit what you're feeling as well, what happens next?

The essays that follow are long entries directed at this question, but I will give you a couple of very short ones here, so you can get a sense for what I'm after. Just a few weeks ago, as I was writing the final chapters of this book, I was in a talk at Georgetown University, in the business school. After the talk, a retired professor came up to me and asked about my university affiliation. He said he once attended a BYU football game in the afternoon and then a University of Utah game later that night.

"That's a lot of football," I told him. But he wasn't talking to me to bring up the football.

"Are you from Utah?" he asked. I could tell that he didn't really care where I was from.

"Northern Arizona," I said. "You wouldn't have heard of the town." That was enough of a clue.

"You're Mormon?" he said.

I answered in the affirmative. And then it was my turn to ask a question to which I already knew the answer. "Are you a Christian?"

Two or three questions later, he was telling me about his doubts. Though a longtime member of Philadelphia's oldest African American Episcopal church, he personally held Arian sympathies. "Me too!" I told him. During the academic talk we had just left, we had nothing in common. I knew nothing about business practices in Western Africa. He wasn't interested in my philosophical views. But just minutes afterward, we were talking over doubts about the incarnation. I wish I had asked him why he felt the way he did. I feel like he would have wanted to explain.

Second story. During the height of the pandemic, I was the only person in my department still working in the office. As the summer wore on, I eventually gave up any pretense of professional respectability. On one occasion, I walked out of my office to use the photocopier right before joining a Zoom workshop with colleagues from other schools. Returning a moment later, I found my door had locked behind me. Not only had I left my keys in my desk, but my glasses, wallet, phone, and shoes were inside the office too. I made a quick lap of the floor. No one was there. I stumbled up a few floors to the dean's office, where a single light was on at the reception desk. I glanced at my watch: two minutes till my meeting started. Rounding the corner, I heard Taylor Swift's *Folklore* playing loud enough for anyone in the office to hear. The album had just been released a couple days before, and I too had played it nearly continuously. A single student worker sat at the desk.

"Hello!" I began, out of breath. She looked startled by the sight of another human. Although, without my glasses, who knows exactly what her expression conveyed.

"Are you OK?" she asked.

"You're listening to *Folklore*!" I declared.

The student brightened. "I am!" she agreed.

"What's your favorite?"

"Betty," she said.

"The best answer!" I was enthusiastic. "Listen," I said, "I'm supposed to be in a meeting in about 30 seconds. I have locked myself out of my office and have no ID, phone, glasses, or shoes. Can you help me?"

She smiled at me with a slight, confident nod. "Plenty of time," she said.

◆ ◆ ◆

Here is an overview of the book. Chapter 1 is my first set of dispatches from Mormon Zion. These are stories about life in Utah County. They are also about making something real by imagining it. Joseph Smith described Zion as a place built by humans and then taken up to heaven by God. It was a heaven made on earth. Something similar can happen in the life of an individual person. Think of a time when you aspired to develop a value that you didn't have already. Maybe you've wanted to come to appreciate the nuances of art or classic movies or fly tying or even religion. Agnes Callard says that when you aspire to gain a value (e.g., appreciating classic movies), you must act despite not yet having that value. After all, if you had the value (already appreciated classic movies), then there's no need for aspiration. You fully possess the value already. And if you never came to have the value, then your aspiration would have failed. Successfully aspiring to a new value, then, involves pursuing a quality of appreciation that you will have in the future but don't yet have. It requires that you see your future self as the ideal version of you, and that is what motivates your current self to get there. Your imagining the ideal gives you the reasons to get to it. Mormon Zion is like that, but for a group of people.

Chapter 2 is a story about fly-fishing in downtown Provo on a Saturday in early March, the first warm Saturday of the year. Chapter 3 is my second round of dispatches from Mormon Zion. Zion is also supposed to be about freedom. But all the concept of Zion furnishes is the idea of sharing a heart and sharing a mind. How could that make anyone freer? The first step in my answer is to borrow a theme from anthropology, via an essay by David Velleman. We follow the ordinary way of doing things, because we're limited by our concepts. We just don't think of other possibilities. Second step: Imagine that you have religious commitments that stop you from doing what would otherwise be ordinary. You would have to find ways of thinking of new options. And adding options—expanding the range of choices meaningfully available to you—is what freedom is about. So, in a roundabout way, I suggest that Zion can be the land of the free in more or less the way that the earliest Latter-day Saints always wanted.

Chapter 4 is about reading Taylor Swift in Utah. In particular, it considers a set of Swiftian ideas about how you can shape the person that you are. Your self is something you make, yourself.

Chapter 5 is a story about my mom. The aim is to think about the kind of relationships that become available to you if you face other persons directly—that is, if you talk to them as if you had a close personal relationship, even if you've never met them before. That is the kind of relationship that Zion is about. The model for this is Jesus. Also, I tell the story of a wild raccoon and a twentysomething conservationist.

Chapter 6 is about fly-fishing, again. This time, the claim is that it's always surprising how different our values are from those of people around us. We can all be doing the same activity, and yet our values can all be very different. That isn't a problem. It's just the way things are.

Chapter 7 tells stories from the classroom. Most of the time (in my experience), the only identity common to students and teachers rests in their complementary roles within higher education. At BYU, however, everyone at least potentially has another source of common identity. Can Zion come to class?

Chapter 8 is about a talk I heard in church in Provo, Utah. The question posed by the talk is, Why does God sometimes tell us things that don't make sense? The bigger background question is, How does it change your life if God is a part of it? Mormon Zion isn't just about sharing heart and mind among humans. God is there too. How does that matter?

Chapters 9 and 10 describe two ways of dealing with the arbitrariness of religious life. Religion gets rid of some actions that are ordinary to others, but then it sets up some new, ordinary actions. From an outside point of view, these might not make sense. Why follow the rituals and practices of *this religion* rather than those of some other religion?

One answer comes from Charles Inouye. Charles has served in a variety of leadership callings in various Latter-day Saint congregations everywhere he's lived, throughout his entire life. But he has been influenced also by Buddhist writings and practices. His solution to the "Why this religion and not another?" question is to refuse it. There is nothing wrong with bringing Buddhism into Mormon Zion.

Chapter 10 is about my dad. He has, likewise, worked in the church his entire life. He's tithed his entire life, attended weekly meetings, and all the rest. One day, around ten years ago, I was passing him in the hallway, and he mentioned—offhand—that he wasn't "a very religious person." His point was that he didn't understand much of the reasoning behind the religious practices he knew so well. His solution to the "Why this religion and not another?" problem was to refuse it in a different way. One may have no reasons for this religion rather than another, but that's also fine. There's nothing wrong with being committed to something arbitrary from the point of view of having reasons.

◆　◆　◆

The big picture view of this book is that Zion—or Mormon Zion anyway—is a phenomenon made by humans. But to say that it is "made" does not, of course, imply it is constituted by physical facts. It isn't. It isn't even made of institutions or conventions or anything else that you might observe through the usual methods of social-scientific inquiry. I couldn't promise you that any respectable social science could detect Mormon Zion at all. In that sense, Mormon Zion is invisible. What, then, could I say to the skeptic who thinks that the whole idea is made up—that there is nothing that constitutes Mormon Zion in any physical or metaphysical way?[6] For the most part, the skeptic has got me. My only defense is that Jesus says the same about the kingdom of heaven itself, so at least I'm in good company. And Zion is only a forerunner to that kingdom. The work of making Zion is the work of taking time and effort to see others the way they see themselves—or, maybe, to see the persons they *want* to become. That may not quite get us to seeing their thoughts or feeling their emotions, but it's something.

In 1835, Eliza Snow foresaw building a Zion that "would like Eden bloom" in the desert. From there, she anticipated the return of Jesus, the Saints rising immortally from their graves,

---

6. For what it is for one thing to "constitute" another, see Karen Bennett, *Making Things Up* (Oxford: Oxford University Press, 2017).

and Zion spreading to the entire Earth. That was how it started. Far be it from me to say how it's going. But for my own part, having lived in Utah County for nearly a decade, I have encountered at least something of what Snow hoped for. Thank you to Alan and Meagan, my all-time favorite neighbors, who made their home feel like my home too. Thanks to Cate and Jared, with whom I felt a shared point of view from the first time we ever inhabited the same church meeting, and to Kif and Stirling, who welcomed me to Utah and included me in their lives. Thanks also to Heidi and Paul, Quinn and Maren, and to Mike, Kara, Jessica, Adam, Carlee, Brock, and Jessica. I first moved to Utah in 2013 for Terryl Givens's Summer Seminar on Mormon Culture (a.k.a. Mormon Camp), which remains among the most memorable religious and academic experiences I've had. The last day, Terryl said a specific thing he had learned from each of the thirteen participants, a practice I've tried to remember in my own teaching. The two people who most dedicated themselves to helping me find my way in my new home were Kelly, my faculty mentor, and Caitlyn, the best TA of any TA I have ever had, been taught by, worked for, worked with, seen, or been. Thanks to Jess, who encouraged me to write folklore (which this book isn't, but still). Thanks to the best office on campus, especially Krista, Carina, Lindsey, and Grant. I'm grateful to Bryant and Taryn, who accepted all my complaining with warmth and friendship, and to Kyra and Sam Bostwick, who shared their own magical home with me. I'm grateful to my editor at Eerdmans, Andrew Knapp, for his enthusiasm and support for this project and to Jenny Hoffman for getting it through the production process. I'm also grateful to Derek Keefe for his careful and extremely helpful editing of the manuscript. And thanks to those who read and responded to earlier versions of the manuscript: Lindsay Brainard, Jane Davis, Rachel Finlayson, Jessica Flanigan, Terryl Givens, Tim McKeon, and Kelly Patterson. To all these people, and also to the persons who appear in the essays that follow—Dave, Megan, Laurie, Carey, George, Terryl, Mie, Rachel, Brendan, James, Lindsay, Ian, Jamie, Adrienne, Quin, Brad, Luke, Rozlyn, Xander, Hadley, Shoe, Andy, Julia, Charles, and, most of all, Jane and Terry, my parents: if I ever see you again, it'll be Zion to me!

Millennial Imagining

Outside my apartment building in Provo, Utah, a 1999 Dodge Voyager is parked on the street. Its license plate reads MIL-FLCN. From the looks of it, the minivan's decade and a half of service has taken its toll. On my walks back and forth from school, I always hope to cross paths with its pilot. "You drive that!" I'd say, gesturing to the considerable dent in the passenger side sliding door. "You're braver than I thought!" And then there's a galaxy's worth of potential follow-ups. "What's your best time in the Kessel run?" "How's the smuggling business?" Running my hand over the damaged rear fender: "The Empire hates this minivan!" Or if I saw the driver parallel parking next to the building, I would nod approvingly but then caution: "Great, kid. Don't get cocky!"

I've yet to meet the owner of MIL-FLCN. But passing by it each day, I wonder, "What kind of place is this?" Every place has its own peculiarities, of course. Utah County has perhaps the highest density in the entire world of members of a church who self-identify as a "peculiar people." The settlers who found their way here had set out to build a "Zion in the mountains," an American millenarian fulfillment of ancient prophecy. Zion, in their imagining, was conceptualized somewhat minimally as "the pure in heart" (Doctrine and Covenants 97:21), where everyone is "of one heart and one mind." The abstraction of their destination makes more sense when you allow that—with a few exceptions—they had seen it literally only in vision.

Chapter 1

So, did they build it? On the one hand, the question seems absurd. Contemporary Utah—with problems as mundane as anyplace else—is hardly imagined by anyone, contemporary Latter-day Saints included, as the millennial Zion that Deutero-Isaiah, or even Jedediah Grant, might have had in mind. At the same time, those early pioneers definitely built something. It wouldn't be crazy to expect some telltale signs of their cultural inheritance, some two centuries later. For my own part, I want to avoid either the triumphalism of lazy religiosity or the empirical confidence of armchair sociology. The Saints' home was supposed to "blossom as a rose," not be seen through rose-colored glasses. Neither would fit with the aspirational ideal anyway.

With all those caveats in mind, I'll speculate that maybe, in a small way, they did build Zion—perhaps a little by accident. Those early Saints created a social world that rules out a lot of otherwise ordinary values in the present day. This is nowhere truer than in late adolescent life. My conjecture is that closing down those options forced people to find new ways of imagining how to relate to each other. And sometimes, those new ways of relating can let perfect strangers catch a glimpse of each other's hearts and minds. Inadvertently or not, they made something not too far from the Zion the early Saints had hoped to usher into the world.

I make no pretense of providing evidence for such a bold conjecture. My method, instead, will be philosophical anthropology. I will look at just a few cases to learn something not about the world but about a concept, the concept of Mormon Zion.

September 2014

My first year teaching at BYU, I walked home on a Friday evening around eleven. Stopping for a red light, I turned to see what looked like a large object slowly moving toward me. Nearly a block away, I could make out the outline of what appeared to be a sofa. Yet it was moving at a steady clip, as if carried along just above the sidewalk. Puzzled, I sat through two lights in the darkness awaiting the sofa's arrival at my intersection. Finally, it emerged from the shadows and joined me beneath the streetlamp at the intersection. And there it was, just as it had seemed: a fully operational moving couch. Someone—the driver, I presume—had had the idea to take an ordinary sofa and install it on top of a similarly ordinary electric scooter. As the couch joined me within my cone of light, a young couple seated together came into view. They waved at me cordially. I nodded my approval back to them, and they proceeded north along University Avenue without saying a word.

February 2015

Working the BYU library one evening, I was quietly interrupted by a student who had approached my desk. I looked up from my book. "Yes?" I said.

"Sorry to bother you," the student offered. Followed by: "Would you like a chocolate chip cookie?"

"Absolutely, yes," I said. It was still warm. I intended to praise the student's work as far superior to the standard BYU fare to which I was accustomed. (There are many events at BYU that involve free cookies, so I know our university's standard-issue cookie quite well.) Before I could comment, the student was already on to the next table, offering cookies to a happily per-plexed study group. Moments later, another student appeared at my desk, gesturing at a gallon container of milk she had in tow. She offered me a plastic cup. "Why yes!" I said again. "It so happens a glass of cold milk is exactly what I wanted just now!"

For the slightest instant, it struck me as some kind of miracle. BYU is very proud of its creamery, which offers a variety of distinctive flavors of milk. This was the sort of small level, sugary, bureaucratic largesse I had come to believe in as a BYU employee. There's even a "mint brownie" milk, combining two of BYU's signature offerings.

After a second, however, I realized the two students must be confederates in some larger plan. As they were about to leave my area, I went up to offer a quick thanks for their thoughtfulness, but also to investigate. Were they part of some organization or something? They responded that they were not, and then—with considerable evasion—one of them suggested that they had just thought that maybe "tonight was a night" when people working in the collections could use a cookie. I accepted their explanation, and they went off in search of a deeper floor in the library's basement.

What was so special about tonight, I wondered? It wasn't midterm exams. Why would people need a treat? I consulted my calendar. *It was Valentine's Day.* The young cookie couriers had wanted to brighten the day for those who might have—putting it delicately—not had much going on, and where better to find such persons than the depths of the library stacks? Their slightly obscure way of responding to my question belied a thoughtful aversion to calling attention to those facts. I looked down the hall with the thought that I might catch up to them, but they were already out of view, off to find some other solitary studiers who might or might not know what day it was.

December 2016

When I arrived at the department Christmas party, I stopped in where the student employees were sitting. "How are things at the cool kids' table?" I asked no one in particular. I nodded to a couple of spouses whom I had been introduced to before. Rachel gestured to her plus-one for the evening, a woman with dark, curly hair sitting next to her. "This is Erin," she said, adding to me, "Erin's my best friend." Rachel then turned back to Erin, "This is the guy who wrote that essay on Taylor Swift."

"Wait a second," I said. "You actually read that essay?" Taylor Swift was a standard office talking point between me and Rachel. We both had been fans since the beginning, agreed (at the time) that *Red* was her finest album, traded theories about what her next reveal would be, and so on.

"We've talked about this essay before," Erin added.

I clutched my heart through my suit jacket. "You got your *best friend to read my Taylor Swift essay!*"

Rachel waved me off with a slight smile. "We go through a lot of Taylor content," she assured.

"It was a good essay!" Erin offered.

I looked from one of them to the other. "This is the most meaningful thing anyone has done for me this year," I declared.

Rachel laughed. "Says something about your year."

"And what a great year it's been!" I insisted.

"Well," she said, "merry Christmas."

"Merry Christmas!" I replied.

Interlude

Zion was first imagined among the Latter-day Saints in 1830. Mere weeks after the publication of the Book of Mormon, Joseph Smith began dictating a revelation about prophetic figures from the Old Testament, starting with Genesis. Picking up on a single cryptic line about Enoch, the father of Methuselah in

Genesis 5, Smith developed an extended version of the story. In his retelling, Enoch built a glorious city whose inhabitants were so righteous that he receives personal assurances from God. The city is "blessed upon the mountains, and upon the high places, and did flourish" (Moses 7:17). In Smith's version: "And it came to pass that the Lord showed unto Enoch all the inhabitants of the earth; and he beheld, and lo, Zion, in the process of time, was taken up into heaven. And the Lord said unto Enoch: Behold mine abode forever" (7:21).

Genesis 5:24 says that "Enoch walked with God; then he was no more, because God took him." In the retelling, it is not just Enoch but the entire city that God takes. The suggestion seems to be that the city had found a way on Earth to live according to the principles of heaven. It's important that it wasn't just one person, because here the crucial idea is that the way the people related to each other was itself heavenly. In a soteriological reversal, God sees that a group of people had assembled themselves as a heaven, and so, "in the process of time," they are "taken up into heaven" as they are. No revisions, no notes. Heaven-on-earth can have temporal and maybe conceptual priority to heaven-in-heaven. Smith reiterated the relationship later in life, saying, "the same sociality that exists with us here will exist among us there" (Doctrine and Covenants 130:2).

What is that sociality supposed to be like? In Joseph Smith's retelling of the Enoch story, the concept of Zion is stated explicitly: "And the Lord called his people Zion, because they were of one heart, and one mind, and dwelt in righteousness; and there was no poor among them" (Moses 7:18). A related definition is given in Doctrine and Covenants 97, in which God promises his presence in a temple the Saints would build. There, the "pure in heart" would see God. The passage then gives the definition, "for this is Zion—the pure in heart" (97:21).

These sound like demanding standards, even if their content is not entirely clear. It would be a lot for two separate people to be of one heart and one mind, much less an entire city. At the same time, there does seem to be something appealing about it. What does it mean to share a heart, or a mind, anyway? Olivia Bailey, a philosopher, writes, "People have a complex but profound need to be humanely understood."[1] She proposes that this need can be met; people can share in one another's emotions. It's natural enough to engage in a kind of "imaginative transporting" into another's situation. When you know someone who has just lost their job or suffered the death of a loved one, or, on the other hand, someone who has just gotten engaged or been admitted to their dream school, you can imagine what you would feel if you were in their place.

Bailey underscores that this is "not a cool, intellectual enterprise." You have to get your heart into it, and your heart has to meet the other person's. If the person we're considering is experiencing grief, then our own emotions should follow: feeling a tightening sensation in our chest, feeling pangs of sorrow, and so on. You don't just imagine that you're feeling the emotion. You actually feel it.[2] At the same time, you have to keep in mind that the situation you're responding to is not the actual situation you are in but is the actual situation someone else is in. It's possible to fail at empathizing with another person both by feeling nothing of what they feel and by feeling it too much—getting lost in the fantasy of it.

Joseph Smith's American Zion brought together an entire city of converts from disparate religious traditions. Their expectations varied about everything: worship, community, the

1. Olivia Bailey, "Empathy and the Value of Humane Understanding," *Philosophy and Phenomenological Research* 104, no. 1 (2022): 50–65, https://tinyurl.com/3cxyfrfz.
2. Bailey, "Empathy," 53.

presence of God, about Joseph Smith himself. In trying to hold together a single community in the presence of very different expectations and practices, Smith found himself in a common predicament for new, rapidly growing religious groups. This includes first-century Christians.[3] In his letter to the Romans (widely seen as the most important statement of his religion), Paul confronts the problem of disunity between that portion of Israel who believe in Christ (including himself and other Jews who accept Jesus) and the part of Israel that doesn't. What's needed is God's action. Borrowing from Isaiah 59 and 27, Paul holds that "out of Zion will come the Deliverer; he will banish ungodliness from Jacob. And this is my covenant with them, when I take away their sins" (Romans 11:26–27). For Paul, God would take the conditions of disagreement and resolve them into unity. How? That part is a mystery (Romans 11:25). But God would do it. And it will come from Zion. So, Joseph Smith's Zion concept did get something right, at least in terms of conceptual continuity. He wanted the same thing Paul had wanted. Zion is about replacing discord with unity.[4]

Zion represents a way of working backward from a hope in the future to a transformation of the present. If you and I know, prophetically, that you and I will mysteriously reach a unity of opinion sometime down the road, then however much we might be at odds now, it seems like there's still reason for us to stick together. Knowing we'll agree down the road might just change how we think about each other in the present.

Zion is a place where people share one heart and one mind. We might not share the same emotions, but we can imagine that

---

3. For a high-altitude comparative history, see Robert Wright, *The Evolution of God* (New York: Back Bay Books, 2010).

4. Konrad Schmid and Jens Schröter, *The Making of the Bible: From the First Fragments to Sacred Scripture*, trans. Peter Lewis (Cambridge, MA: The Belknap Press of Harvard University Press, 2021), 219.

we do. And in that imagining, we can succeed at sharing the same emotions in a relevant sense. We might not share the same beliefs, but we can imagine a time when we will. And in that imagining, we can come to think differently about each other in the present. I don't know if that amounts to purity of heart, but let's call it close enough for Mormon Zion.

July 24, 2019

My favorite holiday is Pioneer Day. Officially, Pioneer Day commemorates the Saints' arrival in the Salt Lake Valley in 1847. In practice, it's a sequel to the Fourth of July, coming three weeks later and involving another round of summer barbecues, picnics, and fireworks. But Pioneer Day also involves a fair amount of cultural self-skewering. It offers the chance to lean unabashedly into stereotypes of Intermountain West Mormonism. There are stick-pulling competitions (by legend, one of Joseph Smith's favorite games). Children can race each other with handcarts, sometimes carrying a cargo of younger children. There's an old cowboy who sits in front of Provo's Pioneer Village next to a sign inviting passersby to ask him anything about the city's history. You get the idea.

Since arriving in Provo, my goal has been to win the Provo PIE-oneer Pie Bakeoff, one of several annual contests. Several years ago, I was calling the town office to register for the event, and the young worker there told me she worried that not enough people were going to sign up. I commiserated with her fear. It wouldn't count as a real victory if I didn't have enough opponents. There was even a risk that the bakeoff could be canceled altogether. I told her I would help recruit a few fellow bakers.

The week leading up to the competition, I practiced a few different pies before settling on an apple-bacon-pecan recipe.

It was an unorthodox choice, but you want to stand out to win these things. The competition was judged by a panel that included the owner of a local bakery but also the mayor and the reigning Miss Provo. In other words, it's about one-third baking skill and two-thirds having a memorable idea. Using cookie cutters, I topped the cake with a pie-dough version of the Salt Lake Temple in the center of cookie-cutter versions of the sun, moon, and stars, roughly dividing the top of the pie into three layers. I entitled my pie "Pecans (not quite) without Number." In Joseph Smith's retranslation of the Genesis story, God appears to Moses, who is "caught up into an exceedingly high mountain" (Moses 1:1). From there, Moses has a vision of the world. He sees everything; the whole history of the Earth is somehow wrapped around his vantage point. And in a way this makes sense, since Moses is now looking down from God's own point of view, and the Lord narrates the events that unfold before them both. Unable to process it all, Moses asks his divine guide what is going on. The answer comes back to Moses, "Worlds without number have I created" (Moses 1:33). When the Latter-day Saints arrived in Utah, they preserved a reference to the celestial vision on the outside walls of the Salt Lake Temple, which includes images of the sun, moon, and stars.

I'd say my pie was high on concept and middling on more bakerly virtues. But I decided it was better than my other ideas: "Celestial Marshmallow" and "Pie to Kolob." For the sake of narrative momentum, I won't explain either of those.

Finally, the day arrived, complete with its pioneer dress-ups, picnics, contests, photo-ops, and all. I brought my pie to an outdoor stand in the center of the festivities and surveyed the competition. Laurie, the one person whom I had persuaded to participate along with me, was there with her "New Jerusalem Pie," which consisted of baklava cut cylindrically so it could be baked in an ordinary pie tin.

"I'm not sure they'll count this as a real pie," she told me. It had a small flag with its name planted in the center of the baklava, so judges would be sure not to miss the wink in her idea. (Latter-day Saint scripture envisions a "New Jerusalem" to be built in America [3 Nephi 20:22; Ether 13:3-6]. Laurie described her entry as a "pie for the New Jerusalem, with a taste of the old.")

"This is exactly the spirit of Pioneer Day," I told her.

A small gathering of friends drifted over from other areas of the festivities to see the results: a family from my ward; a couple of friends from the BYU law school; and Carey, my friend from grad school and Laurie's sister. They offered their good wishes—as if they might cheer my pie into crossing the finish line ahead of the others.

The winners of the pie contest were set to be announced at high noon, right after the conclusion of the Utah County root-beer-chugging competition. A little after noon, a City of Provo employee announced that Miss Provo would be declaring the victor. In keeping with the ethos of her religious upbringing, her short speech assured all contestants of their worthiness and underscored the difficulty of the task she and her fellow judges had been called upon to complete. With bakers' egos suitably comforted, she read off the winners. Third place went to a cherry pie with ornate latticework, a classic, well-executed choice. Second place was an apple streusel pie, delicious and paradigmatically American—core Pioneer Day values, both. Miss Provo then paused, glancing up at the maybe thirty or forty people who had drifted over from other parts of the park.

"And in first place," she said, lingering a beat for suspense, "Ryan Davis, for his Black Lava Pie!"

My friends' kids cheered. Someone got out a phone and started filming. Carey laughed just slightly, as if startled by a twist in the day's plot. I was floating down to the announcer's stand on the glorious cloud of hometown triumph, almost within arms' reach of the trophy. For all of about four seconds, I inhabited fully the joy of winning. But just as Miss Provo was extending her hand to congratulate me, a questioning thought pushed through the haze of victory into the clear sky of conscious attention: Black Lava Pie? My mind insisted on repeating the words, and then on hearing them as a clear malapropism for *baklava*.

"I'm afraid there's been a confusion," I confessed to her. "The New Jerusalem Baklava Pie is actually from Laurie Batschi."

Miss Provo didn't miss a beat. "Correction!" she announced into her microphone. "In first place is Laurie Bat . . . shee!" The crowd cheered again. In hasty retreat from the podium, I passed Laurie halfway back to where her family was standing. She laughed with a shrug; I saluted. A moment later, back in the circle of onlookers, Carey nodded her head, first to one side and then the other, in a spirit of equanimity.

"More layers to this than your average pie."

"I'd say the whole thing went just about as well for me as it possibly could have," Carey surmised.

"I might say the same of my own values," I agreed. She looked at me as if in question.

I thought about it for a second. "Now that I've said it, it might just be true."

Carey nodded, encouraging. "That's what matters."

June 2013

I didn't grow up in Utah County. My first week back in Provo as an adult, I had lunch with James and Lindsey. Our paths had crossed in grad school, and James and Lindsey were both finishing law degrees. They were natives, and their families lived in the valley still. I asked them what it was like living in the very heart of our religious tradition.

"You've never lived in Utah," Lindsey asked me, "not even for school?"

"I didn't go to BYU," I told her. "What is it like?"

James intervened: "Have you ever heard of penny tapping?"

"No idea," I replied.

James loved a good story. He relayed how kids in Utah County would sometimes sneak up to a neighbor's house after dark and tape a penny to the window. They would then attach a string to the penny and back slowly to the nearest concealed location. Suitably hidden, they would then pull the string to tap the penny against the window. When the puzzled inhabitants would finally emerge to see what was going on, the mischief makers would slip back into the suburban night.

I was suspicious. "Is this real?"

"It's really a thing," Lindsey agreed.

"Huh," I said. "What an interesting practice."

That very night, reading in my apartment, I heard the slightest tapping noise against my first-floor window. Outside I found the telltale string, discovered its connection to a quarter taped to my window, and backtracked across the sidewalk to a patch of bushes.

"James?" I asked. "Lindsey?" I paused. "Are you guys in there?"

No one answered, and so I followed the string to the other side of the bush, there coming face to face with two similarly surprised teenagers. They looked like maybe high school seniors or first-year college students, either of which would make sense given my just-off-campus apartment.

"Where's James?" I asked them. "Did he put you up to this?" They stared back at me, unsure if they were in some sort of trouble.

Chapter 1

"What are you talking about?" a boy in a baseball cap asked, glancing nervously at a blond-haired girl next to him. I briefly recounted my lunch from that day, James's story, and how I assumed that he must be managing their mischief. Again I was met by blank stares.

"So, really you just happened to pick my window, no connection at all to James or Lindsey?" I queried again. They nodded in unison.

"Huh," I said, fascinated. "So, what happens next?"

They exchanged nervous glances, as if uncertain whether I was threatening to turn them in to some authority or inviting myself to join them for the next stage of their mild hijinks. I couldn't tell which prospect worried them more.

"Nothin'," the boy in the baseball cap said with a shrug.

"That's it?" I asked, disappointed.

"That's it!" the girl affirmed, relieved.

"Well, Godspeed to you," I offered. They waved uncertainly and retreated across the street.

In the decade since, I've never encountered or heard of any other penny tapping in Utah County. James and Lindsey deny any complicity.

Conclusion

Can you imagine your way into a kind of community with others? Zion is the hope that you can. You might have to picture things in a way that you know they are not or to imagine yourself in another's position so as to feel a part of what they're feeling. Or you might see yourself disagreeing with someone at first but then coming to agree with them, and then proceed to treat them as if your imagining were the truth. Being part of a religious community in the fallen world is about faking it till you make it to heaven, and Zion is the in-between step. It's after separating oneself from Babylon but before getting taken up to God's kingdom. It's before the eschaton but after the apostasy. It's the not completely faking it but also the not yet having made it. In the space left in between, the ways you and I have imagined ourselves in the world are—almost—recognized in turn by each other as the truth, as real. Zion is a place where you can console a person you've never met or encourage a stranger you won't see again. You can act as if you're friends and so make it the case that you *really are* friends. You can enlist others in an activity that has never crossed their minds before. You can make it an event or a party or a date. Zion elides the difference between aspiration and reality. It's where a 1999 Dodge Voyager can be the Millennium Falcon.

CHAPTER 2

I Don't Fish on Saturdays

I don't fish on Saturdays. On Saturdays—without work or school or church—the rivers are crowded. And fishing is a zero-sum game. If someone else has been down the river before you, you are not going to catch the fish they caught. My father always said that you should never fish on Saturday if you can help it.

Yet it was Saturday, and I was on the river. Worse, I was on the river in the middle of Provo on the first warm Saturday of the spring. Today was the only time that Dave could go. He had the baby for the morning while Anne was at rehearsal. Looking through his apartment window at remnant Wasatch snow fading under the noon blue sky, he mused that it would be an easy walk down the bike path by the river, parking the stroller while taking a few casts from the shore. He liked to think about what was possible. I didn't suppose he meant to do it.

"If you want to, I'm in for it," I said.

He shrugged. "Now is as good a time as any."

We started at the Walgreens parking lot. A thin layer of brush and trees lines the city stretch of the Provo River, giving the illusion of wilderness. A bike path winds along the entire length of the river, from where it tumbles out of Provo Canyon to its final meandering into Utah Lake, a couple miles below us. On spring's first seventy-degree weekend, the city had emptied into the parks and playgrounds thoughtfully placed along the river's wider bends. We walked single file with the stroller so the skating teenagers, cycling families, and jogging college students could get around us. Dave continued a short way downstream while I took up casting into a pool under the bridge, noticing a few brown trout sunning themselves in its depths. Not long after I began, one of them inhaled my hare's-ear nymph. After a few jumps, I pulled the 13-inch trout up the concrete embankment, just as a couple of other anglers were walking by. They stopped to watch as I dropped the fish back into its pool.

"How'ya doin'?" I asked.

"Pretty good," one said. "We must've had fifteen between us from the lake to here."

Fifteen trout that I wouldn't catch. I gestured to the soft plastic lure fastened to the guide of his spinning rod. "The 3-inch Gulp Minnow is a good bait," I said. I wanted to think he looked a little concerned at my discernment. Probably not, though.

"What are you using?" he asked. "Bead head hare's ear." I showed him the fly, and we wished each other luck.

I found Dave standing in a small break in the brush line, casting his Panther Martin upstream in a small pool. I noticed a trout turn in the sunlight. "There's one above you and to your right," I advised. He flung the spinner upstream, reeling it back with the current. It didn't look right. The Panther Martin is meant to be fished downstream at an angle, its concave/convex blade pulsing in tension with the current. Fishing it upstream, you have to retrieve faster to make the blade spin, pulling it up out of the pool and away from the fish.

Time goes fast on the water. We moved from one opening to another, arriving at a park with picnickers setting up a barbecue. Dave looked at his phone, shading it against the sun.

I felt bad that he hadn't caught any. "Want to try the fly rod?"

"I ought to get goin'. The baby will need to eat soon." He showed no sign of disappointment.

"OK," I said. "I'll walk back a ways with you and maybe then give it another try back where we started."

He glanced up at the mountains, sharply framed by the city's edge and the clear March sky. "What a great Saturday!" he said. "For the first time, I feel summer comin'."

◆　◆　◆

By the time I was back to the parking lot at Walgreens, the first signs of shadows were creeping across the bridge. The walk had been longer than I expected and had included a stop for sandwiches.

Benefiting from my polarized glasses, I could see a few trout hanging lazily in the pool, moving just slightly from time to time to snatch up one of the tiny midges drifting by. As I walked down the short trail, an older man passed me.

"You catch the fish!" he said. I thanked him for his encouragement. He smiled approvingly. I got down to the river. A young couple in matching outfits walked up to the head of the pool and spoke briefly with each other. A photographer came next, setting up a shot of the couple with the river as backdrop. On a Saturday in Provo, you can bet that someone is planning a marriage. I wondered about getting out of the frame, but they didn't seem concerned. The next time I looked up, they were gone.

A small girl came by, the brake on her purple scooter squealing as she pulled off the bike path.

"Can I watch you fish?" she asked, without introduction.

"Fine by me," I replied. "I don't think it will be much fun. I haven't had any luck since I've been back here."

She had sat down at the top of the bank, behind me. I watched her to make sure she was clear of my backcast.

"I've always wanted to go fishing," she said. "I always wanted a fishing rod. But my dad says they are expensive. But maybe I will get one next year. But so far I haven't ever been fishing. It seems fun though. Sometime, I would like to try it."

I looked back at her. She glanced from me to the fly rod and back. "OK," I said. "Come give it a cast if you want, but I don't think we are going to catch anything."

By the last half of the sentence she had jumped into the river and held out her hand for the rod. I managed to suggest that she return to shore, where I began giving her instructions about how to cast a fly rod. Like riding a bike, you don't think about it when you know how, but learning how can be unintuitive. I confirmed she was right-handed and situated the rod in her hand.

"Now, gently move the rod back, stopping just behind your shoulder, and then . . ."

She was ignoring me. Once I took my hand off the rod, she flailed the tip back toward the rocks behind us and then jerked it forward. The fluorocarbon leader snapped, sending the fly out into the brush. I glanced anxiously at the Sage five-weight's delicate tip, relaxing as I saw that my six-hundred-dollar rod was spared.

"Let's try a new plan. I will cast, but if we hook a fish, then you can reel it in." As I said it, I remembered the Lewis River in Washington state, a vast torrent of a stream in my mind's eye. On its banks, my parents had once struck a similar bargain with me, and my saying the words brought to mind the only other time I had heard them spoken.

"Besides, we need to try a new place anyway." My companion acceded easily to my request, seemingly indifferent to casting anyway. I always assume people want to fish because they want to *fish*. No number of counterexamples makes it less surprising.

She pointed downstream.

"Let's go to the other side of the bridge and try there," she said. "I've been riding around here all day. My sister too. She is somewhere around here. I don't know where she is right now. How long have you been here? Have you been fishing the whole time?"

The girl seemed intent on filling any silence. I looked at my phone. 4:23. "I was out this morning. I came back after eating lunch."

"So, you've been here a few hours. Me too. I have been here more than a few hours, actually. This is a good place to come on Saturday." She kept talking.

I would guess she might have been in the fourth grade, although it is hard to say, not having measured the sizes of elementary school children in some time. Her cheeks had a kind of glitter that could be seen when her face caught the sunlight. She was physically slight but spoke confidently, always in complete sentences.

Her small size and apparent fearlessness gave me the idea that she might have absconded from some supervision. "Are you sure you are OK being out here alone? Do your parents know you're here?"

"Oh, yeah. They like it when I come here. My sister is here somewhere. I am not far from home. I can get there on my scooter in five minutes. Let's go to the other side of the bridge and go fishing. I will look for some fish."

She was on her scooter again, yelling "wheeee!" as she sped down the path, below the bridge, vanishing on the other side. I climbed out of the stream and followed, half expecting that she would be gone by the time I reached the pool. Instead, she had dismounted and was peering into the stream.

"I see a fish," she said, pointing to the pool. "It's by that shopping cart!"

Sure enough, a 15-inch brown trout was resting in the small

space between the concrete wall and a sunken, moss-covered shopping cart.

"Cast over here!" she insisted. "The fish is here!"

She kept up her descriptions as I placed a few casts around the pool, glancing up now and then to receive acknowledgment that I was following her stream of thoughts. A trout—this time a rainbow—came out from the shadows, its blueish back flashing as it opened and closed its mouth. I set the hook.

"There is a fish! You have the fish! The fish is on your line!" Her voice rising with each exclamation, my partner apprised me of what was happening. As I moved to hand her the rod, the line went slack, and the size 18 hook slipped from the rainbow's mouth. It was gone.

I worried she might be saddened by the loss. It was always so discouraging for my much younger self when a fish slipped away before my father managed to get the rod to me as I paced the bank, waiting.

"Sorry about that," I offered, but she looked indifferent about the event, again staring into the pool, blocking the sun from her face with the back of her hand.

"Oh, it's fine. The other day I flushed a Doritos bag down the toilet," she said.

I offered that we all make mistakes. She nodded vigorously.

"Well, I had been eating them in bed, but no one knew I had them, so I had to find a way of getting rid of it so that no one would know. But then the toilet stopped working. A man had to come and try to fix it. My dad says we were almost thrown out of our apartment this time. *Fortunately* [she emphasized the word], they fixed it. But now I guess my Amazon money is gone."

I was looking at her now. I had guesses of my own—about what her apartment looked like, what her room looked like, how her father might look. She told the story just as matter-of-factly as all her other declarations. It seemed to her just to be a series of events, a narrative of sorts, but nothing beyond that. Still, I felt like I should try to say something comforting. "Everything you did sounds pretty reasonable to me." It was a feeble effort, I thought as I was saying it.

She shrugged. "Kids will be kids," she sighed.

I laughed out loud, and she grinned at my reaction. "I don't know if you are in a good dialectical position to be the one saying that." I didn't expect her to be paying attention.

"It *is* funny for me to say that!" she agreed. I laughed again.

"Another fish!" She was pointing back at the pool now.

For the next half hour we worked the pool, spotting fish and casting to them. I was getting a little concerned that someone might be missing this small person, but I had nothing to go on but her assurances that she was fine. We even hooked another fish, but lost it as we had the first. Again I was forgiven freely. Again she peered into the stream where the trout had been. Her eye caught another flash of blue, this time an old Bud Lite.

"Look!" She pointed. "It's a beer can! Like the ones my dad has." She bent down as if to reach for it.

I wanted to coax her back from the concrete ledge. "I bet whoever threw it in there drank it first," I said.

"Yeah, I think it's empty."

"Probably it's full of river water."

"Of course it's full of river water!"

Shadows stretched across the pool now. The evening had a slight chill, as spring evenings do. I figured she must be getting tired. I told her I was going to go down the stream a little way, as if to indicate that we might part company. She agreed that this was a good plan. She was back on her scooter now, her tiny foot pushing against the bike path with the force of her entire body.

"Wheeeeee! This is SO FUN!"

She was referring to her scooter now, having just come to a long downhill coast, accelerating as she put both feet on the scooter. I didn't expect her to stop again, but she did, waiting for me. I told her I was going to walk through the brush to get back to the river, suggesting it might be too rough for her to follow. She countered that it was no problem at all. She walked through the brush all the time. We reached the river, and I mumbled another farewell of sorts. I pointed to the other side and said I was going to cross. She nodded. I waved and began to wade across. Behind me there was a splash, and I turned just as she was finding her way onto a rock above the cold water.

"What are you doing?" I asked.

"Aren't we going to fish the other side?" she said.

"Well, I don't think you can make it. This is a pretty big river, and you are a small person." I told her she might fall in, but she shook her head emphatically.

"I will be fine. I weigh almost fifty pounds!" She would definitely not fall in, she assured me.

"Have you ever fallen in the river before?"

"Never!"

It occurred to me that she might be getting the better of me with this answer. I followed up: "Have you ever waded in the river before?"

She was forthright. "Nope." There was no hint of guile.

By then I was walking back toward shore. "I don't think you should wade to the other side."

"Are *you* going to wade to the other side?"

She knew that she had me. I could tell. I looked back to the pool across the stream. The dark-bluish tint of the water revealed its depth—a good home for a large trout. It was out of reach, given my circumstances.

The baby. The image of the pool at which I had found Dave in the morning returned to my mind. The baby was why he didn't go upstream and then cast the Panther Martin back down-stream. He didn't want to leave the baby alone by the bank.

"Are you going?" The girl was asking me again.

"No. I'm not." I was defeated.

"Good thing!" She was happy I had seen the wisdom of not crossing. "That was too much work for a lousy old fish anyway! And you would have probably fallen on your behind. And I probably would have been swept away in the river."

I gave her a quizzical glance, which she did not register.

"Well," I said, "that would have been embarrassing for both of us."

"Embarrassing for you," she countered. "For me: terrifying! Being swept away by a river is too scary to be embarrassing."

"You have me there," I admitted. "That *is* how those concepts work." She nodded confidently, apparently pleased at having won a concession.

"Where should we go next?" She was on her scooter again.

Maybe I would go home, I told her. After all, we had both been out for hours now, as we had established.

She looked up and caught my eye, smiling a little, as if plotting. "Or," she paused, "we could go to 7-Eleven—and get some snacks!"

For a moment, I considered this. She had been out all afternoon, burning energy like a hummingbird. She was wire thin, probably hungry. And it had been hot all that time; she had no water bottle. I glanced at her, and for the moment she said nothing. On second consideration, the plan seemed impossible. I could not just take someone else's child, whom I had met just hours ago, to 7-Eleven. What was her name, anyway? There was no point asking now.

My thought was broken by some other kids riding past us on bicycles.

"Well . . . are we going to 7-Eleven?" she asked. It would be wrong to say she was prodding. She simply wanted to know. Only now she had the slightest note of urgency.

"I don't think we should," I said. She showed no disappointment. "I'm going to go play with those kids," she said.

"Happy Saturday!" I told her. She was already on her way, picking up speed on her scooter.

Visions of Freedom

As a young man, Charles W. Penrose converted to the Latter-day Saints, turned down a nice job in the English government, was promptly disowned by his wealthy family, and found himself with nothing. He planned to emigrate to Utah but instead was called to proselytize his new religion in England. After five years of work, Penrose, poor and exhausted, anticipated finally leaving to join up with his adopted people in the Western United States. He had started having dreams of the Great Basin. He described being able to see the Saints' gathering place clearly in his mind.[1] En route to a meeting, he stopped and composed his image into a poem.

> O ye mountains high, where the clear blue sky
> Arches over the vales of the free, where the clear
>   breezes blow
> And the pure streamlets flow, how I've longed to your
>   bosom to flee!
> O Zion, dear Zion, land of the free
> Now my own mountain home, unto thee I have come
> All my fond hopes are centered in thee.

1. Kenneth W. Godfrey, "Charles W. Penrose: The English Mission Years," *Brigham Young University Studies* 27, no. 1 (1987): 118.

Penrose wrote these words in Essex. He had lived his entire life in England. He had never seen a mountain, at least not the Utah variety.

I first heard this story as a nineteen-year-old, when I was myself just starting out at the Missionary Training Center in Provo, Utah. The moral of the story seemed to be that if you were a little homesick at the prospect of serving a two-year mission, things could definitely be worse. In the MTC version of the story, and this may be apocryphal, Penrose had just received word that his mission had been extended for the third time by Brigham Young. He would again have to push back his journey to join the Saints. In that moment, he sat down and wrote the song. In the end, Penrose preached in England for ten years before ever having the chance to see the place he had imagined in his mind.

To my ear, the most poignant lines in the verse are the final ones. The penultimate line's perfect tense suggests the writer's presence already in Zion. The final line betrays that idea. It redescribes Zion as the center of his hopes. And you don't usually express a hope for something you have already. Even Hobbes recognized hope as conceptually tied to a lack of the thing hoped for.[2] Can it make sense for your home to be a place you've never seen in real life?

Perhaps Penrose's imagining of Zion was so vivid as to make it true that he had already made his home there. Perhaps he had what the Book of Mormon calls "a perfect brightness" of hope (2 Nephi 31:20). The mountains' clear breezes and pure streamlets were, to him, the markers of home, more than the English countryside of his physical acquaintance. It's common enough to encounter a place, perhaps even for the first time,

2. Thomas Hobbes, *Leviathan, with Selected Variants from the Latin Edition of 1668*, ed. Edwin Curley (Indianapolis: Hackett, 1994), chap. 3.

and find that there's *just something* about it. The way the air feels, the sounds and smells, maybe the way people treat you there, make it home at first sight. So understood, home is less in the geography of one's origin than in the habits of one's action. Home is where one feels security and assurance, the unthinking confidence of knowing intuitively what should be done and said and what should be left unspoken and unfinished.[3] To know how to act without having to deliberate about how to act is to experience one's own agency as coherently integrated. At home, there's nothing stalling or, worse, paralyzing the flow of thought from mind to action. And that, as Penrose exults of his own mountain home, is a kind of freedom.

How can Zion make one free? Suppose you could realize a community of one heart and one mind. Would its inhabitants also enjoy freedom? And, if so, why? My aim in this chapter is to think about how trying to maintain empathetic relationships with people who are otherwise strangers could help to allow one to experience one's own agency as more free. In less philosophical terms, my aim is to make sense of how a place like Zion could feel like home—even if you've never been there before.

September 2016

In the summer months, the department is mostly quiet. With September, life returns to the office. As I was standing over the copy machine waiting for a job to print, a colleague I hadn't seen in a season passed by and then paused and looked back at me.

"How are you doing, Ryan?" he asked.

I looked from him to the copier and back. "Good!"

---

3. See Samuel Scheffler, *Equality and Tradition: Questions of Value in Moral and Political Theory* (Oxford: Oxford University Press, 2012).

"You must have enjoyed being able to spend time with Mie in the summer," he said, optimistically.

Mie and I had been living in different states as she finished her graduate work and I started at BYU. But, more recently, we had also been living in different states because our marriage was coming to an end.

I considered his question. There might have been a way out, but it wasn't worth looking for one, I decided. "We're getting divorced," I told him, fearing the wave of discomfort my words would sweep across the room.

My colleague frowned. "Oh, that's not good," he said.

"It's fine," I assured him. "She's doing fine. I'm doing fine. It's fine!"

My colleague didn't seem to want to accept my rejoinder. But we also were at a conversational impasse of sorts. "Well," he said, exhaling, "I'm glad you're OK, I suppose." He glanced down at his papers and walked out of the office area, down the hallway.

Everyone was silent. It would be impossible not to listen to our conversation. I hadn't told Rachel or Brendan—then working at the front desk—about my marriage. "Well, I'm getting divorced" is never the sort of sentence that it makes sense to bring up out of nowhere. Rachel was close to getting engaged, and Brendan was recently married, so it felt unfair unloading such freighted news on them during what was, hopefully, a happy season of their lives. I retreated to my office.

A few minutes later, I heard the faintest knock on my door, which was slightly ajar.

"Yes," I said, turning my chair around to face the entry. Through the sliver opening, I could see the outline of Rachel's face.

She opened the door just enough to glance inside. "Hey!" she began, then continued, "I'm sorry." Her eyes moved uncertainly toward the ceiling, as if this was as far as her plan took her. But then she went on, more confidently, "I mean, sorry we're always talking to you about stuff, stopping you from getting work done . . ." She paused, as if to allow her sentence to be finished as either a statement or a question.

"You're a good friend," I said back.

"Yeah," she nodded, affirmatively.

"And I would much rather talk about Taylor Swift than political science!"

"Well," she said, "you know where to find me."

"I do," I replied.

She waved slightly through the crack in the door before letting it fall shut.

Interlude

Mormon Zion is meant to make its inhabitants freer than they were before. What would that look like? Here's a proposal: it looks something like *changing what's ordinary.*

David Velleman writes that "no matter what we do, we are doing something else in addition, namely, being ordinary."[4] Velleman's point (which he is borrowing from the sociologist Harvey Sacks) is that we consider only a very small number of the options that are in principle open to us in any given moment. The cognitive processing limits of our minds are such that we can pay attention to only a few potential actions out of the nearly limitless set of things we are physically able to do. Our physical capacity to act freely dramatically outpaces the set of things it occurs to us to do. As Sacks puts it: "There is

4. J. David Velleman, *Foundations for Moral Relativism* (Milton Keynes: Open Book Publishers, 2013), 23.

an infinite collection of possibilities, of things to do, that you could not bring yourself to do. In the midst of the most utterly boring afternoon or evening you would rather live through the boredom in the usual way—whatever that is—than see whether it would be less or more boring to examine the wall or to look in some detail at the tree outside the window."[5]

Velleman thinks through the example of the boring afternoon. There are plenty of "ordinary ways of doing 'being bored'—flipping unseeingly through an old magazine, staring unhungrily into the fridge," etc.[6] When you're bored, those are options that occur to you. Staring intently at a tree or examining nuances in the details of the wall—those are not options that will occur to you. Of course, nothing is stopping you—at least nothing physical. And individuals can sometimes invent new ways of doing things. What you can't do, Velleman says, is "invent an entire ontology of actions from scratch."[7] The problem is that action is conceptually laden. None of us can perform an action for which we have no concept, so the actions available to us are limited by the concepts we have.[8] If I've had a tough day, you could extend friendship or comfort to me by, say, calling or sending an encouraging text or even ordering me a tasty dessert. Those are ordinary things to do. But you wouldn't hang a freshly fallen maple leaf from the inside of my refrigerator with the lyrics to my favorite Taylor Swift song handwritten on the back. However much I might delight in the gesture, it's just off the conceptual menu of actions for the situation.[9]

---

5. Quoted in Velleman, *Foundations*, 23.
6. Velleman, *Foundations*, 23.
7. Velleman, *Foundations*, 27.
8. On the connection between concepts and action, see Jonathan Lear, *Radical Hope: Ethics in the Face of Cultural Devastation* (Cambridge, MA: Harvard University Press, 2008).
9. Until now, that is!

The ordinariness of what we do comes with important benefits. First, doing what's ordinary allows others to interpret our actions the same way we do. And this is because of a shared sense of appropriateness. If we all know the cultural scripts we're following together, then what we do will be intelligible to each other. I can do what's ordinary for professors to do, and my students can do what's ordinary for students to do. Our compliance with the templates helps our actions seem appropriate to each other. Even if it occurred to you to hang the maple leaf from my refrigerator, you might have second thoughts. You might wonder: "Is this weird? How will this look?"

A second benefit is efficiency. Doing what's ordinary means you don't have to invent every piece of your action. You go to a wedding or a funeral or a graduation and can pick the cards, the gifts, the clothes, even the expressions of emotion, that match the occasion. We construct chains of action with what Ann Swidler calls "some pre-fabricated links."[10] Acting from scratch all the time would be exhausting.

But there is a downside. Because all of this ordinariness is, well, ordinary, it doesn't reveal too much about us as persons. How often have you forgotten every single thing that was said to you for your birthday, or struggled to write a wedding card that conveyed literally any feeling that you yourself had actually had in connection with either person being married? It's a commonplace that sometimes when you love someone, you appreciate their flaws. One explanation is that it's in the small failures, rather than the successful actions, that we get a glimpse of another as a person—that we "really see them."[11]

But now imagine that for some reason a whole slew of the actions culturally available to you were somehow off the table.

10. Quoted in Velleman, *Foundations*, 27.
11. I talk more about this in the next chapter.

Try to imagine a world in which all of the scripts for the roles you inhabit were unavailable. You go to speak some words to the cashier at the grocery store, but for some mysterious reason the first thing that comes to mind is something you can't say. And then you can't say the second or third things either. What would you say then? Now, suppose it wasn't just with the cashier as they were scanning your cereal and milk. Imagine the same thing happening at school, at work, in the library, and so on. What kind of things would you do, and what would your actions communicate to others about you?

My armchair sociological conjecture is that, at least in some small way, this is what's happening in Mormon Zion. Imagine a college town of 30,000 undergraduates where the two things you absolutely cannot do are drink alcohol and have sex. These prohibitions don't just rule out two possible actions from an otherwise limitless horizon of possibilities. If we take these two rules for granted, what does that do to the meaning of social relationships, making plans, going out, Friday nights, Saturday mornings, and so on?[12] In a contemporary American college setting, these two prescriptions take out prefabricated action links that structure a variety of potential intentions. And, to be honest, these are just the most conspicuous of the rules and almost certainly not the most consequential.

Do me a favor and grant me (for the sake of the argument) the premise that Mormon Zion rules out a lot of what would otherwise be ordinary. What then? Of course, that vacuum will immediately be filled by something else. Ordinariness is like the air we breathe. And I don't have to tell you what's ordinary

12. I'm not so naïve as to think everyone does take them for granted. But still, many do. What's distinctive about Mormonism, which various surveys have shown, is the remarkable compliance with such prohibitions. Of course, that's not to valorize those who do comply or criticize those who take a different approach.

about Mormon Zion, because that's the part you already know—the styles, the hair, the way of talking, Mitt Romney. My point is not that there isn't an ordinary but that now—and maybe especially in college—ordinariness has a few cracks in it. There's space for actions that don't usually appear on the cultural menu of possibilities. Add to this a religious identity that insists all your coreligionists should think of each other in a familial way, right down to replacing the standard Mr./Ms./Mrs. titles with Brother or Sister instead. Your faith makes it OK to talk to strangers as if you're already familiar, which puts on the table a set of prefabricated action links usually unavailable. At the same time, it has a bunch of rules that take off the table a set of prefabricated action links that are usually ordinary. The result, at least in the best case, is pressure from two directions to let people see more of who you are than they otherwise might.[13] I'm not saying it's making people better or worse, just different. Or, to put its differentness in a different way, it's making a *peculiar people*.

What do we have now? An argument, at least approximately. And it goes something like this:

1. People can be either ordinary in the usual way or ordinary in a slightly different way.
2. Mormon Zion rules out some of being ordinary in the usual way.
3. If people are ordinary in a slightly different way, then they'll see more of each other's humanity than they otherwise would.
4. Seeing more of another's humanity than you otherwise would has its costs but also makes possible relationships of greater empathy.

13. Are there cases where it goes wrong—cases of not-in-the-best case? Absolutely. Zion is, as always, aspirational.

5. Relationships of empathy are what Zion is made of. (This was the point of the last chapter.)
6. So, Mormon Zion helps make Zion.

This essay hasn't done anything fancy, but the argument has gotten a bit unwieldy in its moving parts. I certainly haven't said something here to convince you of it. But I'm not out to convince you of anything. Whatever that would look like, it wouldn't be Zion.

◆ ◆ ◆

The Latter-day Saints imagined their westward migration as a modern American exodus. They abandoned Nauvoo across a frozen Mississippi River in the dead of winter on a (misinformed) rumor that federal authorities were about to move against them. That admittedly lacks a bit of the original's flourish. A rumor from a former postmaster general is less cinematically inspiring than hot pursuit by Pharaoh's war chariots. And fleeing across an ice-covered river might not instill as much confidence as walking on dry ground between parted walls of the Red Sea. But it's still dramatic enough that the story has wound its way down to my own lifetime. As a child, I could recite the story about how the Mississippi so seldom froze hard enough for transit by wagon that only an act of God could explain it.

The modern exodus narrative only gets better from there. The Latter-day Saint settlers then faced an expansive desert. On the other side was a promised land they had seen literally only in vision. The geography of that promised land could hardly invite clearer comparison with its biblical model: a long valley with a river flowing north from a large freshwater lake, emptying into an expansive salt sea. They called it the Jordan River, of course. And although they didn't exactly expect that crossing it to enter their own promised land would set in motion God's apocalyptic plans, they still had in mind that they—like the first Christians—were living in a millennial moment. Moses got just to the edge of the promised land. He lived out his final days on Mount Nebo, just within sight but unable to enter. The Saints named the southernmost peak in the Wasatch Range—just within sight of their promised land—Mount Nebo. But, unlike Moses, nothing stopped them from forging ahead. They formed settlements all around it. To the north, Salem. To the south, Ephraim. Beyond that, on the outskirts of a barren desert, Moab.

Utah has its own version of Mount Sinai: Ensign Peak. From there, Latter-day Saint leaders surveyed the valley in 1847 and decided that it was where they would raise their "ensign for the nations" (Isaiah 11:12). In so doing, they would complete the job that Moses himself had miraculously given to Joseph Smith a decade before (Doctrine and Covenants 110:11).

Of course, of all religious peoples who still read Isaiah, only the Latter-day Saints—with a particular combination of literalism and optimism—suppose he was talking about building a Zion in the mountains of the American West. Whatever one makes of that claim, there is one thing the settlers of Utah did share in common with the exiled Judeans returning to Jerusalem. As encouraged by the writer now called Deutero-Isaiah, a prophet or anonymous collection of prophets, those early migrants were promised wondrous events. The details of these events were modeled on great New Year celebrations in Babylon.[14] Zion would be like that, only grander and more miracu-

---

14. Isaiah 40:3-4. See Konrad Schmid and Jens Schröter, *The Making of the Bible: From the First Fragments to Sacred Scripture*, trans. Peter Lewis (Cambridge, MA: The Belknap Press of Harvard University Press, 2021), 113.

lous. In other words, their beliefs about the Zion to which they were returning were not based on any memories available from their own lifetime. Those representations were, inevitably, based on the materials they had seen. From those, they imagined Zion, a place they had never been.

Some twenty years after finally arriving in Utah, Charles W. Penrose was speaking at the Salt Lake Tabernacle on a Sunday afternoon in July.[15] His address ranged over a variety of subjects, but in the final few minutes he talked about building Zion. He still described it through a kind of imagining. Only now, knowing Utah well, he didn't give his own imagination's rendering of the high mountains and clear streams. He focused, instead, on Isaiah's imagining. Penrose quotes the following text from Isaiah 2: "And it shall come to pass, in the last days, that the mountain of the Lord's house shall be established in the tops of the mountains, and shall be exalted about the hills; and all nations shall flow into it. And many people shall go and say, Come ye, and let us go up to the mountain of the Lord."[16]

Penrose recounts that the Saints were then doing everything as Isaiah had foreseen. They were building a temple in the tops of the mountains. They had built the Salt Lake Tabernacle, in which they were at that very moment assembled (which, he suggests, Isaiah had also envisioned). And people were coming to Zion from all over the world. Penrose says, "Those who receive the Gospel come in here 'as doves to their windows.'"[17] Though he doesn't mention it, Penrose's reference is to Isaiah 60:8. In that chapter, the prophet sees Zion being built again, people

---

15. Charles W. Penrose, "Divisions of Modern Christendom—Effects of Sectarian Proselytism, Etc." (discourse, Tabernacle, Salt Lake City, Utah, July 17, 1881), *Journal of Discourses Online* (blog), Joseph Smith Foundation, accessed March 21, 2023, https://tinyurl.com/4ar4f8ym.

16. Penrose, "Divisions."

17. Penrose, "Divisions."

returning, carried there in ships with sails like clouds. How exactly they are like doves returning to windows is not entirely clear. But I like to imagine that, at least in Penrose's mind, they were arriving to a new place in the way that one might return to a familiar place. That is, they were coming to Zion in the mountains in the way they might be going home.

Early March 2016

Utah Lake has been a popular fishing location since before Mormon settlers even arrived in modern-day Utah County. In the 1840s, the lake was home to native Bonneville cutthroat trout, left over from Lake Bonneville, which once encompassed much of contemporary northern Utah. Spanning from what's now the Idaho border in the north, extending beyond contemporary Provo down to Sevier County in the south, the pluvial lake offered a niche for its own species of predatory trout, the Bonneville cutthroat. When Mormon settlers first arrived, Bonneville cutthroats still inhabited the lowest reaches of the valley, a bizarre fact for anyone who's seen the warm, murky waters of today's Utah Lake. Most of the biomass is now made up of common carp, a fact that conceals a more surprising, prized quarry. Early every spring, before the higher elevation snows have even begun to melt, walleye materialize around Utah Lake's tributary streams. Among the best known of these is the Provo River.

Starting from its headwaters in the Uinta Mountains, the Provo descends through pine forests and then meadows to meet Jordanelle Reservoir. To that point, the river is really a small freestone stream, holding a few large trout in its deeper pools but mostly the domain of small brook trout and mountain whitefish. Between Jordanelle and Deer Creek Reservoirs, the middle section of the Provo flows through affluent Heber Valley, where its mostly small, wild brown trout are fished by vacationing anglers out of Park City. Below Deer Creek, the lower section of the river tumbles through Provo Canyon and finally winds its way through the cities of Orem and Provo, finally emptying into Utah Lake.

Many people fish the river at each stage, though you'll meet different kinds of people along the way. Although *upper, middle,* and *lower* refer to the elevation of different sections of the river, they work almost equally as well as designations for the social class of the fishing population. In the upper and middle sections, anglers wear the finest waders, cast conspicuously labeled thousand-dollar (often more) fly rods, and scrutinize sophisticated fly boxes to locate what they take to be the most precise offerings. In the canyon section of the river, one may still encounter the odd black Escalade in the parking lot, but the most common angler is now the weeknight Utah County dad taking a few hours to fish after work. Toss in a smattering of college students and their obliging dates, and a seasoned angler here or there looking for a trophy brown trout, and you'll know more or less whom to expect around any bend. In town, you'll still see a fly rod or two, but here the river is fished mostly by suburban teenagers and older folks just looking to pass a few hours along the bank. Finally, at the mouth of the Provo, one will meet the anglers least prosperous in money but—with few exceptions—richest in fish catching.

At the mouth of the Provo, walleye represent the greatest and most elusive prize. They run up the river to spawn, appearing only at dusk and, even then, only irregularly. I first encountered the walleye spawning run a year after moving to Provo. At the mouth of the river, I noticed a line of some fifteen or twenty anglers, standing only a few feet apart, casting repeatedly into the deeper pool where the river's turbulent current settled into the lake. Though they appeared to be catching nothing, they had the look of a group waiting for something to start. I turned off my pickup on the long dike extending into the lake, and for a while I watched them. Just as darkness was settling, as if being swept in by the chill spring wind from off the shore, one among their group had his rod double over with a fish.

"Walleye! Walleye!" A whooping shout went up. The angler brought the fish to him, standing chest deep in the water, and placed it into a metal basket tethered to his waders. It was a large fish, easily over 20 inches.

The next night, I was back at the mouth of the Provo, wearing my own waders, rod in hand. I eased down into the final section of the stream, the sun hanging over the opposing mountains to the west. I was early, but there were already a few fishermen in position. I motioned to a man upstream, seeking permission to wade up into the water below him. He smiled and beckoned me over. Over the next hour, the regulars arrived in ones and twos, till eventually we had formed a line extending down the pool at the river's mouth. A few of my fellow anglers looked at me, affable but perhaps a bit perplexed.

Without warning, the walleye arrived in the river. Some twenty yards above me, someone hooked into a fish, sending a cheer down the ranks. Moments later, my own offering was seized by a fish, and after a fight I pulled the 23-inch walleye alongside me in the stream. My neighbor to the west held up a large net floating beside him, gesturing to my fish. I waved him off with a thank you, explaining that I could just as easily keep the fish in the water. Hemostats in hand, I gently pulled the hook from the roof of the fish's mouth and slid the fish back into the river.

"What are you doing!" my neighbor yelled at me.

"I'm sorry?" I asked.

"YOU DROPPED THE FISH!" he exclaimed, as if he could only interpret my behavior as some kind of mistake.

"I'm a catch-and-release guy," I tried to explain.

"Give the fish to me!" he invited, as if—again—this was the obvious thing to do.

Here I should clarify that my commitment to releasing the spawning walleye was, if not my single deepest moral commitment, at least the one about which I was most often exercised. I didn't explain it this way, but I find the urge to keep large fish just as baffling as my fellow angler found my desire to release them. A spawning female walleye might be nearing a decade old. Keeping such a fish deprived the river of a natural treasure. It also undermined the reproductive cycle making such fish a possibility in the first place. I wasn't above calling the DNR to report violators of state maximum limits, an effort I had already undertaken more than once when I saw people carrying walleye out from the Provo.

I shook my head. "I put the fish back!" I said. My counterpart threw up his hands in exasperation, shaking his head as if to say that he *knew* I put the fish back but just couldn't comprehend *why*.

The next night, the twenty us of were back at the river again, and again we caught a few fish, and again when my turn came, I released it back into the depths. Someone shouted at me.

"No!" he said. My neighbor of the night before sighed and said something to his comrade. I got the sense that it was about me but not meant for my hearing. If so, they rightly guessed that my high school Spanish would be insufficient to discern their exchange. He ended with a wave of the hand to his friend. The gesture was not so much to excuse me as to communicate that it was no use reasoning with me.

A couple of days later, seeing me put yet another walleye back into the river, my neighbor asked me, "You fish for fun?" I nodded. He shrugged again, disapproving. He looked up at the sky as if in search for some heavenly witness to my foolishness.

The next night, a cold offshore wind blew white caps into the riprap shoreline adjoining the confluence of river and lake. The shallow water was easily pushed into heavy rollers by the wind, and the threatening weather—along with the fact that the spawn was winding down—left me unmotivated. I sat in my car and resolved to grade papers until I saw someone else catch a fish. No point getting wet and cold for nothing.

I kept an eye on the river while half-heartedly reviewing midterm essays. The regulars began to roll in, parking their cars along the dike and donning their waders and jackets. (I regularly wore a life jacket when the waves pushed against the shore, but no one else bothered.) I had settled back into my reading when I heard a hand pound against the hood of my pickup.

"It's time!" my neighbor yelled.

"No es ahora!" I called back to him, pointing to the sun still well above the mountains.

He laughed but shook his head. "You fish!" he insisted, gesturing from me down to the river below us.

"Trabajar," I replied, uncertainly, holding up my stack of papers. "*You* fish!" I waved at him as if to push him down to the lakeshore.

He walked back to my driver-side window, gesturing between us. "We fish *together*!"

I shrugged and got out of my truck, pulling my waders out of the backseat. "We fish together," I repeated. A cheer went up from the group. As we picked our way down to the water, a spring rain started. No walleyes were seen that night.

CHAPTER 4

Taylor Swift and
the Metaphysics of the Self

My favorite moment in Taylor Swift's 1989 is a five-second stretch of "You Are in Love," the album's penultimate track. In those five seconds, nothing happens. No words are spoken or sung, and the simple melody nearly disappears. I believe it is the album's emotional climax. Swift's point in that moment, I will suggest, is that absences can be locations of meaning.

That much, I admit, is obvious. Anyone who has ever seen an overture or invitation to another person meet with an initial uncomfortable pause, however slight, knows that silences can tell us something. For that matter, anyone who has ever listened to a Taylor Swift love song knows that what people refrain from saying can matter as much as what they do say. But—to invoke another bit of well-worn Swiftian wisdom—the fact that something is obvious hardly means it isn't worth saying. My claim in this essay will be that Swift's insight about meaning can also teach us something about what it is to be a person. We not only can exercise some control in the meaning of the events that make up our lives. We also can, thereby, have some say in deciding who we are. The self is an object of its own construction. And that is part of why each individual self is a someone worthy of love.

◆　◆　◆

Chapter 4

Like many a Taylor Swift song, "You Are in Love" is a story. And even if you have never heard it, you already know what the story is about. Still, details matter, so I will rehearse them. The song opens with its protagonist entering her bedroom after a date. It's dark. She's alone. It's been one of those magical whirlwind evenings—as rare in real life as they are common in Swift's musical imagining. The protagonist tries to remember exactly what happened, and her memory rushes through a series of images. Buttons on a coat. A moment of laughter. Coffee at midnight. A light reflecting on her necklace. Their shoulders brushing accidentally. Somehow, the sum of the parts doesn't add up to what her experience had been. She has "no proof," but still she "saw enough." She is "in love."[1]

Let's be clear about one thing. It's not enough. We've all had that magical evening with a crush that we then enthusiastically recount to a best friend, hoping that our friend will confirm that the magic we felt was real—was part of the night itself and not merely our own projection onto it. Only our story is met with a kind of cautious skepticism that makes us think we must be leaving something out. Except, nothing has been left out. We may think we're in "love, true love," but really it's a counterfeit made of adrenaline mixed with optimism and youth. (I'm speaking here in the first-person plural out of the hope that this experience is universal.) When we really want something to be real, it's natural enough for our belief to outpace the proof by a good stretch.

In real life, after one of these moments, the odds of relationship success are still long. Never mind that. This is a Taylor Swift song. No one should be surprised when, in the next verse, our protagonist and her lover really do make it out of the woods.

---

1. Taylor Swift, "You Are in Love," track #15 on *1989 (Taylor's Version)*, Republic Records, 2023.

They start a relationship. It becomes public. It has its ups and downs. Still, there is something special. He wakes up in the middle of the night, his face strange. He tells her that she is his best friend. And just like that, she knows he's in love.

At the risk of belaboring the point, I will say what I think is happening in this moment. The protagonist's lover wakes up with a start. Somehow, he's had a realization. There is no evidence from which it follows. Nevertheless, like the good Swiftian character that he is, he speaks now. What he says is, "You're my best friend." But the protagonist hears "I love you." She interprets his utterance thus because she too has been awake in a dark room in the middle of the night, so she recognizes that strange look on his face. And because she knows what he means, he is right after all. Right not just that she is his best friend, although certainly it is in a best friend's job description to know what we mean, even when we say something different. He is right also in what he *meant* to say. He is in love. And because he is right, she was too. It had been true love all along.

♦　♦　♦

I am not finished retelling "You Are in Love," but for a moment I want to take stock. What, exactly, makes it true that one is in love? In what does love consist?

Perhaps these questions sound hopelessly abstract. But I think that Taylor Swift is on to something. Swift takes her own insight to be difficult to put into words, so it should not be surprising if the answers are a bit elusive. In her early albums, the young Taylor Swift identified love with an emotionally charged response to another's qualities or attributes. That's just an arid way of saying that you love someone when you see how great they are and decide that you should be together. On this view, when I fall in love with you, I notice "the way you walk, way you talk, way you say my name," and my noticing makes me want you to notice me in a similar way.[2] This may be the dominant idea of love in much of pop music, including the young Taylor Swift's. Falling in love is mediated by an appreciative response to another person who is exceptional or excellent. You see someone's beautiful eyes or the colors in their eyes or are otherwise arrested by how beautiful they are, etc. Those are all Swiftian ideas, though they of course could be anyone's. To give this analysis a suitably dry, philosophical handle, let's call it the *properties view* of love. You love another person when you respond to someone's seemingly exceptional properties by wanting to be in a romantic relationship with them.

Another popular view about love is that it arises out of a certain kind of shared experience or personal history. On this view, love is the product of time spent together. You love the person who looks over at you in the passenger seat either of an old Chevy pickup (like the pre-famous Swift) or of a Maserati (like the newly famous Swift). Either way, it's the personal history, not the price tag, that works the magic. You find that person who is the only one who can match you in James Taylor records or whose presence gives you that "roller coaster kind of rush."[3] Let's call this the *relationship view* of love.

As I've described them, the properties view and the relationship view differ as to what brings love about, but they also share something in common. On either account, love involves a particular kind of aim. You want the person with great qualities to see your great qualities too. Or you want the person you enjoy being with to want to be with you. The resulting game plan is all too familiar: do what will make the other person like you. And

2. Taylor Swift, "Hey Stephen," track #4 on *Fearless (Taylor's Version)*, Republic Records, 2021.

3. Taylor Swift, "Begin Again," track #16 on *Red (Taylor's Version)*, Republic Records, 2021.

so it is no surprise at all that many hit songs, including many of the young Taylor Swift's iconic hits, had exactly this perspective on the beloved. Young Taylor Swift was jealous of a crush's girlfriend, or at least hoped a crush would find his way back to her door. She insisted, *"You belong with me."*[4] If love is ultimately about getting together with another person, then for any story to be a love story, that other person has to *do* something. Even if all they have to do is "just say yes" to the very idea of a love story itself, they still have to do *something* that you want them to do.[5] And, as we all know, that makes love an intensely stressful business. It is not easy to get another, completely separate human being to do what you want. So, the project of being in love, thus conceived, can be consuming. "All I think about is how to make you think of me," pleaded the teenage Swift.[6]

You might think that although this anxiety is a disadvantage of actually being in love, it is no disadvantage for the properties view or the relationship view of love. Being in love *is* stressful, and so we should want our theories of love to explain that fact. And these theories hold appeal in another way. Our experience of love seems very much directed at the excellences of our beloved, and also to our relationship with the beloved.

All the same, I think that the appeal of these accounts is largely illusory. Although superficially plausible, these explanations of love have a hard time getting the details right. If you love me for my beautiful eyes or hair or my fancy car, then what happens when you meet someone with a better car or superior eyes or hair? If the properties view of love is right, you should love that person even more than you love me. But

---

4. Taylor Swift, "You Belong with Me," track #6 on *Fearless (Taylor's Version)*.

5. Taylor Swift, "Love Story," track #3 on *Fearless (Taylor's Version)*.

6. Taylor Swift, "Invisible," track #13 on *Taylor Swift*, Big Machine Records, 2006.

while trading up for a better model is okay for Chevy pickups and Maserati (I just confirmed that the plural of Maserati is also Maserati), it is not OK for lovers—at least not true lovers. Or what happens if I lose my hair, get Coke-bottle glasses, or wreck my car? Should you abandon a love if their excellent properties diminish in some way? That doesn't seem to be the stuff of love stories either.

Similar problems beset the relationship view, although it will take a little more philosophical creativity to expose them. Suppose you were to wake up tomorrow with global amnesia, unable to remember your past life. Would it then make sense to stop loving your spouse? Not necessarily. Or an even more creative example: suppose you discovered that your entire personal history with your spouse was an elaborate fiction. Still, it seems, you could rationally go on loving that person. In general, we don't usually think that our love depends on relationship history. I might continue to feel love for old friends years after we've lost touch. Or I might feel love for a relative I'd prefer not to see at all. And then there is love at first sight, without any past relationship. Sometimes your eyes whisper with another person across a room, and—just like that—you are enchanted. The Swiftian corpus is replete with these cases. Examples like this glorify everyday occurrences with magical language.

So, if love is not warranted by another's properties or by our relationships, then what does justify love? It might seem like nothing is left. And according to Kieran Setiya, that is precisely the answer. Nothing justifies love. In a recent article patiently canvassing all of the counterexamples that I've described in the last couple of paragraphs, Setiya comes to the following conclusion: "The simplest view to take here, and the one that I accept, is that it is sufficient to justify love that its object is another human being. It would be a mistake to love a baseball card more than I love my child, but there is no one it is irrational to love. Any one of us would be justified in loving any other."[7]

This might sound odd. Certainly, it seems like there might be people that I should not want to be in an ongoing relationship with, especially an ongoing romantic relationship. Shouldn't there be something that justifies love?

This question gets to another important issue for the properties view and the relationship view. According to these accounts, love essentially consists in a certain aim—namely, the aim of being in a certain kind of relationship with another person. But if they are wrong about what justifies love, perhaps they are also wrong about what love involves.

In an influential article on love, David Velleman distinguishes between having an "aim" and having an "end."[8] Your aim in an action is what you want to accomplish or achieve. However, you can sometimes also have an end, which is something that motivates you, but not with an eye toward getting it done. Velleman gives the example that you can go to church for the sake of your dear, departed mother. Although this motivation makes sense, your mother is not something that you aim to achieve. Rather, your mother is an end of your action in the sense that feelings about your mother partly explain your reasons for going to church. In this way, people can be the ends of our action without being our aims. Persons, according to Immanuel Kant, are "ends in themselves."[9] Their value in no way depends on any of our designs or plans.

7. Kieran Setiya, "Love and the Value of a Life," *The Philosophical Review* 123, no. 3 (July 2014): 260, https://tinyurl.com/pmz5bup5.

8. J. David Velleman, "Love as a Moral Emotion," in *Self to Self: Selected Essays*, 2nd ed. (Ann Arbor: Michigan Publishing Services, 2020), 86–136.

9. Immanuel Kant, *Kant: Groundwork of the Metaphysics of Morals*, trans. Mary Gregor and Jens Timmermann, 2nd ed. (1785; repr., Cambridge: Cambridge University Press, 2012), sec. 2.

Velleman's point is that as long as we focus on aims, our theories will fail to capture what love is really about. As long as we think of success in love as getting another person to view us in a certain way or have a certain relationship with us, we will be failing—in a sense—to think of those other persons as ends in themselves. We will instead be thinking of their value as at least somewhat depending on their doing what we want them to do or feeling the way we want them to feel. And that thought is not from love.

So, what is love then? Velleman writes: "I am inclined to say that love is likewise the awareness of a value inhering in its object; and I am also inclined to describe love as an arresting awareness of that value.... I suggest that it arrests our tendencies toward self-protection from the other person, tendencies to draw ourselves in and close ourselves off from being affected by him. Love disarms our emotional defenses; it makes us vulnerable to the other."[10]

To my mind, this proposal gets close to the heart of love. Certainly, love often travels in company with desires for another's affections or company. We do notice the qualities of those we love, and we do remember our experiences with them. But if Velleman is right—and I think he is—then none of these things is love itself. If I care about another person as an end in herself, then I will not think about what I want that person to do or feel. I will appreciate her for herself. When we appreciate people in this way, they can affect us in a way others cannot. That is why we are vulnerable to them.

It might help to have a concrete example of how to go about disarming one's emotional defenses. And this is, I believe, where Taylor Swift's more mature view of love reenters the picture. Consider the prologue to her third album:

10. Velleman, "Love as a Moral Emotion," 94–95.

What you say might be too much for some people. Maybe it will come out all wrong and you'll stutter and you'll walk away embarrassed, wincing as you play it all back in your head. But I think the words you stop yourself from saying are the ones that will haunt you the longest. . . . There is a time for silence. There is a time waiting your turn. But if you know how you feel, and you so clearly know what you need to say, you'll know it. I don't think you should wait. I think you should speak now.[11]

Swift's advice does not want for directness. But neither is its author blind to the dangers. (Indeed, listeners will certainly recall the tales of wincing, stuttering embarrassment that make up much of her earlier records.) Notice that the advice is self-consciously nonstrategic. The thought is not that speaking now is an effective all-purpose means to success in your plans or purposes. The advice instead is that you should speak now, consequences be damned. Without knowing what will happen, the counsel is to make oneself vulnerable to another. If the foregoing philosophical conjectures are on the right track, then when Taylor Swift advises speaking now, she is really coming down in favor of love. No big surprises so far.

♦ ♦ ♦

We are now ready to return to the storybook lovers with which we began. Their achievement, recall, was that they succeeded in making themselves vulnerable to each other. Braving the risks, they told each other what they were feeling in the moments they were feeling it. And they understood each other. Two completely separate humans recognized the value located entirely

11. Taylor Swift, *Speak Now*, Big Machine Records, 2010.

within the other. This is not easy. Iris Murdoch described love as "the extremely difficult realization that something other than oneself is real."[12]

With the news of their success, the chorus of "You Are in Love" is more significant, and so, dear reader, I will entrust it to you. The speaker says "you are in love, true love," and insists that you can "hear in the silence" and "feel it on the way home," and "see it with the lights out."[13]

It's exactly the same chorus as had followed the first verse. She was in love, and he is as well. The chorus, like the rest of the song, is told in the second person. This has long been a part of Swift's narrative practice. She famously writes to specific, named—or slightly veiled—individuals, whom she addresses directly. Even when her story is about some entirely separate person, she will adopt that person's point of view and tell the story from the adopted standpoint. So it has been since her debut album.

Times have changed. Here, Swift does not identify herself as the protagonist but instead as an observer. Having gotten to this point, the bridge gives commentary, again in the second person: *you* can see now why love matters so much. And then the last line of the bridge: "And why I've spent my whole life trying to put it into words."[14] With that line, Swift assumes her usual place within the frame of the song. Only now she is not the protagonist but a kind of coach. A Taylor Swift song is conversational. A sort of musical in reverse, a Taylor Swift song is a kind of singing that feels like it could break into simple

---

12. Iris Murdoch, "The Sublime and the Good," in *Existentialists and Mystics: Writings on Philosophy and Literature*, ed. Peter Conradi (New York: Penguin Books, 1997), 205-20, here 215.
13. Taylor Swift, "You Are in Love."
14. Taylor Swift, "You Are in Love."

chatting at any moment. Every album features a few lines of just plain talking.

Having situated herself to speak directly to the listener, Swift is ready to offer advice. Direct concern for her listening audience is another familiar Swiftian theme. You don't need to read the internet stories about Swift's spending exorbitant amounts of time finding gifts and preparing care packages for her fans to know that she has a big sisterly impulse to offer care and—as the situation requires—encouragement, protection, or counsel. That theme is also right there in her songs. This is someone who dedicated an entire track on an earlier album to the request that her teenage fans be considerate of their moms. "Remember that she's getting older too."[15] Quite a discerning bit of moral advice, really.

So, poised to advise, Swift wants to impress on us the way in which love matters—why she's spent so long trying to put it into words. Now, the chorus again. "You can hear it in the silence."[16] Except, the line plays differently than it had in the previous two rounds. In each of those, there was an echo, "you can hear it in the silence . . . silence." This time, the echo is removed. The line is no longer offered as a description of the protagonist. It is now extended as a personal invitation to the listener. And after the line comes my favorite five seconds of the album, wherein the melody fades and no words are spoken. Having been assured that we can hear it in the silence, we are given the chance. The echo is similarly removed from the next line, which becomes almost a plea. "You *can* feel it on the way home" (emphasis mine). Another pause. Swift's insistence is firm, though barely a whisper. In the chorus's final line, her

---

15. Taylor Swift, "Never Grow Up," track #8 on *Speak Now (Taylor's Version)*.

16. Taylor Swift, "You Are in Love."

voice quavers just slightly, not exactly breaking with emotion in the way that, say, Art Garfunkel's voice trembles at the climactic moment of the studio recording of "Sound of Silence." Rather, her voice moves with intensity, as if by force of will she could dispel any lingering skepticism the listener might have. "You can see it with the lights out."

And then the song's triumphal moment. Swift has been compared to U2 in her ability to really deliver a satisfying, stadium-filling pop declarative. "You're in love! True love!"[17] Her voice holds nothing back. Like the couple in her story, she is all in.

But go back to the silence. Perhaps lacking the musician's trust in her audience, or maybe possessed of the philosopher's impulse to overexplain, I want to linger on what we were meant to hear. It's worth noting that by her own accounting, Swift's insight here is hard-won. She was not always so discerning of the meaning in life's blank spaces. A younger Swift would imagine the moments of not speaking as walls closing in on her—sources of constriction, discomfort, and anxiety. The pauses were evidence that something was wrong, that the other person was somehow far away. "I'd tell you I miss you but I don't know how / I've never heard silence quite this loud."[18]

My point is not that Swift used to panic in the silence, but then with age and maturity she grew comfortable with it. That would make it seem that the mistake in the past was one of mere misinterpretation. But that is not quite right. The relationship in the song I was just describing, "Story of Us," was in fact a failure. Swift's interpretation of the silence was correct then too. The "Story of Us" is a tragedy because it "looked a lot like a tragedy" from Swift's own point of view.[19] The story is a tragedy

17. Taylor Swift, "You Are in Love."
18. Taylor Swift, "Story of Us," track #7 on *Speak Now (Taylor's Version)*.
19. Taylor Swift, "Story of Us."

because that is how Swift tells it; that was how she interpreted all of that not-speaking at the time.

In other words, the interpretation doesn't try to *figure out* what the silence means. It *decides* what the silence means. And Taylor Swift wants her listeners to get that this is a power they too can have. "You can hear it in the silence!" Just try. This is your story, and it will be the story that you tell.

◆　◆　◆

There is a deeper point here about what it is to be a person. The power to decide what events in your life mean is not just a way of saying that you can decide the story of your life. It is a way of saying you can decide who the person is that the story is about. I realize this is obscure, but I don't mean for it to be at all mystical. I will try to explain.

Let's take for granted, at this point, that love is about making yourself vulnerable to another. Speak now, tell the truth, be real. How to do that? What self should you make known? Presumably, the answer is that you should make known your true or authentic self. You should be genuine. But that just pushes the question back a step. People can always question whether the self you are making known is the one that you really are. We can even have such thoughts ourselves. All we can do is come to terms with the skepticism. Everyone is judged with a skeptical eye. We all have our scarlet letters, and though the rumors about them are terrible and cruel, there may be some truth to them. People will keep doubting. In this regard, Swift has at least one thing in common with another famous bearer of the scarlet letter: the more she insists that her confessions are real, the more hearers will perceive her insistence as new evidence for the opposite conclusion.

The ultimate point can't be to persuade others that one's expressions of vulnerability are real. All you can hope to do is change how you see yourself. But that is still something. Recall the young Taylor Swift, the one who thought love was about getting some boy or other to take notice of her. That Taylor was always in danger of rejection. Much worse, though, she was in danger of losing her self. "I'm only me when I'm with you," she sang.[20] If our self-performance so thoroughly depends on another's validation, then it's no wonder at all that we can lose touch with who we are. We can start thinking only about which thoughts we want this other to have about us. We can vanish into our own aims. And, unlike rejection, that is a real danger.

The alternative is to see ourselves the way we see others whom we love: as ends in ourselves. That means seeing ourselves as tasked with deciding the meaning of events in our lives. More than that, it means seeing ourselves as deciding how those meanings fit together in a way that makes us the persons that we are—or, rather, the persons we make ourselves to be.[21]

That there are silences is inevitable. There will always be dark rooms and waking uncertainties and gaps in conversation. We can fear them or cherish them or both. Dan Moller writes: "The boring is intimate. Long, boring silences can make us uncomfortable, but that in turn lets us prove something if we come to accept such boredom. The awkward silence in the car on the way home from the first date is the glorious silence on the way home from the fourth or fifth."[22] Taylor Swift, again by her own account, has been on enough dates to know. She has felt both

20. Taylor Swift, "I'm Only Me When I'm With You," track #13 on *Taylor Swift*, Big Machine Records, 2006.

21. Here again I have a conspicuous debt to essays by J. David Velleman: "Self to Self" (213-51) and "Identification and Identity" (437-74), in *Self to Self: Selected Essays*. I'm also indebted to Christine M. Korsgaard, *Self-Constitution: Agency, Identity, and Integrity* (Oxford: Oxford University Press, 2009).

22. Dan Moller, "The Boring," *The Journal of Aesthetics and Art Criticism* 72, no. 2 (2014): 181-91, https://tinyurl.com/yh3vjkbu.

things on the way home, and we too can feel either on the way home. As the philosopher (and fellow Swift fan) Jessica Flanigan has pointed out to me, we can even change our minds and change the facts right along with them. The silence on the way home from the first date was uncomfortable at the time, but the memory of that awkward silence can itself be glorious on the way home from the fourth or fifth date. What does the silence of the first date *really* mean? It means what we make of it.

If Taylor Swift stands for anything, it's emotional honesty. In that spirit, I will end on a confessional note. In this essay, I've sketched a case for the thought that the five seconds of silence on 1989 offers a real insight about what it takes to love another person. But perhaps you will think I am overreading, or just making it up. I don't think I am, but I admit uncertainty. I can remember the first time I heard "You Are in Love." When the chorus came around for the third time, I was already thinking of one silence or another I had once experienced on a one-time date with the woman whom I would later marry. When I reached the five seconds, it hit me in the way that any song you love hits you the first time you hear it. And, like anyone, I wanted that response to make sense. I wanted my experience to mean something. Does Swift's voice really tremble faintly the last time through the chorus? I do think so. I've certainly replayed it many times. But I am not so confident as to believe there is enough reason for you to be convinced. But maybe, if you have read this far, you'll give it a try. And just maybe, you will have a similar experience. Maybe it is enough?

CHAPTER 5

My Mom, Shoe, a Wild Raccoon, and Being without Guile

For now we see through a glass, darkly; but then face
to face: now I know in part; but then shall I know even
as also I am known.

—1 Corinthians 13:12

My mother may be the most guileless person I have ever met.
I realize this sounds like exactly the sort of vaguely insulting
compliment that people are wont to pay to their parents—and
maybe especially their mothers. It makes it out to appear that
the person in question is devoid of bad intentions, but in so
doing it also casts the person as naïve or passive or, worst of all,
bland. So, let me be clear: my mother is none of these things,
and I have something else entirely in mind. To be without guile
is neither compliment nor insult. Rather than being a virtue or
a vice, guilelessness is just a way of understanding oneself in
a world of other, completely separate agents. And, like other
strategies of self-understanding, it has some advantages and
some drawbacks. Because guile is so pervasive, and its absence
correspondingly rare, the pros and cons of being without guile
are stark. What makes guilelessness interesting, I believe, is

that it makes human relationships both more and less accessible to the person in possession of it.

My aim is to try to understand the concept of being without guile. The way I use the word may not be exactly how other people use it. This essay will be an entry in what philosophers call conceptual analysis. The project of conceptual analysis is not exactly to offer a definition. Instead, it's to give a description of a concept (or the thought we have in mind) that is good enough to allow you to tell whether the concept applies to anything in the world—and, if so, what. It's like a field guide to a concept. It tells you something about how to spot the concept in the wild.

The difference is that this essay will say more about the wild than most philosophical essays do. But it also will say more about some abstract concepts than most non-fiction essays do. I apologize to everyone in advance.

Pragmatics at the Candy Store

My mom looks a lot like any tourist who might visit a candy store in northern Wisconsin on a rainy Saturday afternoon: suntanned and wearing sandals and a "Lake Girl" sweatshirt. The excursion begins innocently enough. My mom has long maintained a practice of buying her visiting children a selection of candies from the local shop. The tradition dates back not just to when we were young but to her own youth, when her father, who died of cancer in the early 1990s, used to buy local candy as well.

The present story starts with my mom declaring her intention to buy me some chocolate. I say she doesn't need to, having arrived at the age where I can afford it, at least financially. She offers a compromise: she will buy chocolates for herself, as well as a couple for me. Then I can buy more on my own. Agreement is reached.

I realize this is not an interesting story. Bear with me for a moment.

Now we're in the self-declared "Country Store." "Can I help you?" the young cashier asks.

Mom: "Yes! I'd like to buy some chocolate. I will choose a few, and then my son will pick two candies that he would like, and I'll buy those also. But then he will tell you some more candies he'd like, and he'll buy those. But I'd like to get the first few ones that he picks. Does that make sense?"

It does not. Out of eager helpfulness, the cashier responds with an enthusiastic affirmation but then pauses perceptibly. He haltingly registers his confusion: "Well . . ." He trails off but catches her eye to signal a need for clarification.

"Oh, sorry!" Mom says, and begins to explain what she's up to: "I guess I just have this tradition of buying candy for my kids, whenever they come up to the Northwoods to visit. It's a small thing, and I know it's silly, but it's just something I like to do."

The clerk is still looking at her. This was not exactly the help he needed.

What's gone wrong? I know writers are supposed to show rather than tell, but my present problem is that no amount of facts about the circumstances can convey to you what I think is going on here. Understanding requires a theory, and theories are not just compilations of data points. In other words, there is nothing I can show you that will give you the idea I have in mind. So, I have to just tell you. Here goes.

Mom was giving a good explanation. But she was giving it from her own point of view. When the cashier didn't understand, she took that misunderstanding seriously—by reflecting on what was puzzling about her actions from her own perspective. Why, after all, did she care so much about tradition? By her own lights, there might not be a fully adequate explanation for that. So, she had to admit that it was silly. Acknowledging the absence of a fully rational account of one's desire is a perfectly good way of coming to understand it.

It's not, however, a way of getting a fifteen-year-old to put some mint meltaways in a box for purchase. The clerk treated the event as a professional one, where our human interaction is mediated by roles—templates for how to act and not act. In this context, the misunderstanding was not about my mother's motivation but about why she was not just pointing to bins behind the glass counter and saying, "Three of these." The clerk understood all of my mom's sentences, considered individually. The mismatch was in their respective understandings of the situation they were in. My mom's answers didn't fit the pragmatic context the clerk expected.

My suggestion is that this is a problem about guile—or, rather, the lack of it. When you have guile, you don't issue words exclusively from your own point of view. You prepare them for your audience, having in mind the idea that their point of view is different from yours. This has the following consequences:

1. What you say to the other person is designed by you to make sense to them.
2. What you say to the other person is not, unqualifiedly, your own representation of what is going on.

We commonly associate guile with deception, and I think we do so because it has these features. However, just because you're trying to present things with the recipient in mind, it doesn't follow that you're deceiving them. (I'll explain this in too much detail later.) Guile involves an element of strategy, but communicative strategy might just as easily be used for the sake of helping one's interlocutor get a fix on the truth. The

"Country Store" cashier was not in a position to take in all the details about my mom's family traditions, so giving those details distracted from the task at hand. A little guile helps people ease into ordinary social interactions. If you don't know someone but you know their job or their age or background, you can say irrelevant niceties that both avoid deeper interaction and facilitate everybody getting what they're after. This is the art of small talk. Guile is the lubricant for small talk in the great wheels of social and economic machinery that, for better or worse, we all inhabit. For this reason, it makes certain relationships both available and comfortable that might otherwise be neither.

The benefits come with a price. With guile, there is an interpretive puzzle. How does the speaker's own view relate to what he says? When a person with guile speaks, he has in mind his audience already. His words reflect not only his own attitudes but his relationship to the audience—what he wants the audience to think, including what he wants them to think about himself. Everything is mediated, and we know that it is mediated. This has the virtue of providing helpful guidance. But it obscures from view the personhood of the guide. Because it's a little about us, we know it's not entirely about the speaker.

Shoe and the Wild Raccoon

I didn't set out to tell you about speech acts in the candy store. The more important story is about Shoe and the wild raccoon. It's possible that the events in the story could happen in other places, but it especially makes sense when set in my mother's native Wisconsin. Her grandfather had built a cabin on a lake in the wet, cold, alternatively beautiful and forbidding region known as the Northwoods. (Although, when he homesteaded in '37, earlier forests had been all but eliminated by logging.)

Modern tourism notwithstanding, the Northwoods even today shares a kind of kinship with rural communities like New Jersey's Pine Barrens or Appalachia. Locals have learned to live with the cultural stereotypes that come along with the solitude and natural splendor.

Denizens of the Northwoods pride themselves on living close to the land. Family gatherings I sometimes (read: only in the summer) attend revolve around discussions of duck hunting, muskrat trapping, and the like. By far the region's most famous and elusive natural prize is the muskellunge. The muskie, as it's called, looks something like a cross between a barracuda and a pike, with a matching personality. Its natural range extends only along a narrow latitudinal corridor. Central Wisconsin's river system gets too warm in the summer, and the lakes of Michigan's Upper Peninsula—only half an hour away—are dominated by lake trout and other cold-water species. My great-great-grandfather's homestead in the Northwoods lies squarely in the heart of muskie country.

Like her family before her, my mother is a noted fisher of large fish. She spends the summer months—both of them—stalking the shallows of northern Wisconsin's natural lakes. In the annual contest to determine the Northwoods's apex predator, the muskie comes out on top more often than not. But every so often my mother will trick one into inhaling one of her bucktail spinners. She carefully returns every captured muskie to its watery home, but the stories are saved forever. They are recorded in the cottage's yellowed logbook, told and retold, and rehearsed on slow fishing days to keep alive the hope that it could happen again on the next cast—or maybe the one after that.

I learned about Shoe and the wild raccoon on one such slow fishing day. A slow muskie fishing day is unremarkable. Muskies are called "the fish of 10,000 casts," and while I've never met anyone who succeeded at keeping track, that number certainly gets at the right idea. Muskie fishing is a vast expanse of nothing punctuated by the rare explosion of chaotic activity. The muskie's appearance is so inexplicable, so seemingly arbitrary, that its pursuers will latch onto any anomaly to try to understand their successes. To offer just one example, muskie hunters will insist that you are more likely to encounter a fish during moonrise or moonset, even if these events are physically unobservable. They will consult lunar calendars to know when the moon is about to come up or go down and will set their alarms to make sure they remember when the moment arrives. As far as I can tell, no one has an especially good theory about why muskies are purportedly more active with the moon near the horizon. The veteran angler will mumble something about gravitational change and lateral lines but then quickly revert to personal testimony. They have seen it happen enough to *know* that muskies bite more "at moon."

There are two things that muskie fishing centrally requires: time and patience. Don't let the latter mislead you. The virtue demanded is not merely a willingness to sit and wait and do nothing for long durations of time. That's not patience but laziness. Patience is the capacity to maintain focus on small details over long stretches of the day even when nothing is coming of it. Where exactly in the weed bed you've been staring at is there a subtle cut or break that might provide an ambush point for a fish? Is the wind creating any creases in surface current that might help position the coordinates of baitfish?

Along with other practitioners of her craft, my mother fishes with what a skeptic might call superstition and the believer will see as discernment. She notices changes in wind direction, observes cloud cover on the horizon, and sizes up the consequences for where the muskie will be on the move. The muskie hunter is vigilant, even when no signs are forthcoming. She has a religious orientation to the natural world, and her faith can weather many fishless moon phases.

Like other devotional practices, the discipline of muskie fishing involves a great deal of silence. Besides a few notes of verbal encouragement here and there, my mom can go for long stretches without saying anything. The day on which my story takes place was a day like that. It was a normal day of muskie fishing, which is to say we caught nothing. As the sun climbed higher in the hazy July sky, we eventually decided to call it a day and returned to the boat ramp.

As we were taking the boat out, we met the twentysomething woman stationed at the boat landing to inspect watercraft for signs of invasive weeds. The Wisconsin Department of Natural Resources (DNR) pays college kids to check exiting boats at most landings to try to prevent the spread of undesirable aquatic vegetation between lakes. The woman stationed at our particular landing came up and greeted my mom with uncertain recognition.

"Jane?" she ventured.

"Hadley?" my mom replied, similarly hesitant.

They proceeded to have a ten-minute conversation. They talked about nefarious weeds clinging to boat hulls but also about the summer, Hadley's family, her plans for fall, and the like. It was the most I had heard my mother say all day.

We hoisted the boat onto the trailer and started on our way back to my mom's family cottage. I watched the deep green forest go by my window for a couple of minutes. "You and Hadley seem pretty tight," I reflected.

"Hadley's fine," came the reply. "The one I'm really close to is her sister, Shoe."

"You're 'really close' to the woman who checks boats for the DNR?" I asked, incredulous.

"Well, Shoe isn't working this year," Mom reflected. "She's up in Alaska now doing something to observe changes in the tundra. It has to do with her major for school. I told her she'd have to tell me when she saw the northern lights. Sometimes you can see them here, but up near the arctic circle, where she is, that's much better."

My mom knew a lot of facts about Shoe's life. Turns out they had started talking about school and realized—a couple of generations removed—they both had attended the same small central Wisconsin college. I pressed the point a step further, wanting to know how they had *discovered* that fact.

"Well," my mom said, thinking, "she mentioned she goes to class in a building that was paid for by a guy I had gone on a date with when I was there, Dave Pontilnic. He was a small guy and really nervous, but his frat brothers made him ask me to a dance because they knew I was nice and I would go with him."

"Wait a second," I said, my pitch rising. "You dated a frat guy in college? Why have I never heard of Dave Pontiac?"

"Pontilnic," my mom said. "And it was just *a* date. I guess he bought a bunch of buildings for the school. Shoe says that he insisted all the buildings be named after him."

I was still trying to put the pieces together. Mom rarely talked about her past. I vaguely knew she had gone to college, where she had studied Spanish. That was about it.

"So," I asked, "you went on *a* date with a rich guy in college. But . . . ?"

"He wasn't rich at the time. After college, he started a company that made picture frames and got a lot of money out of it."

I pressed a finger to my forehead. "Picture frames . . . ?"

"They're always falling apart. His didn't fall apart."

"Deceptively simple," I said.

Mom was content to let it go at that. I pushed ahead. "Let's table this now," I said. "How," I thought through my next query, "how is it that you and Shoe figured out that you both had some strange connection to Dave Potomac?"

"Pontilnic," she corrected. My mom shrugged. "You know— when you're driving in the car, you just get to talking."

Her oblique rejoinder invited still more questions. "So, you and Shoe . . . went on a road trip?"

"Well, nothing too far," Mom answered, modestly. "Just running errands. . . . One time we were out at Thunder Lake Marsh."

Thunder Lake Marsh was, generally, a mosquito-infested expanse of shallow weeds. "What were you doing *out there?*" I asked.

"Finding a new home for a raccoon." She spoke in the tone one might use to point a dinner guest to the whereabouts of the silverware drawer.

"Wait, wait," I stammered. "You were transporting a raccoon— like, *wild* raccoon?" She nodded. You have to have the raccoon with you if you're going to find it a new home, after all.

I was still trying to find my bearings in the story. "Why did you want the raccoon to live at Thunder Lake Marsh?"

"Well . . ." Mom ruminated, "you have to get them a long ways away, or they'll just keep coming back to their old home." She went on in some detail about how even if a raccoon doesn't know where you dropped it off, it can still figure out how to get back to the place where it lived, even if that place is miles away and it has no obvious trail to follow.

This wasn't exactly the explanation I was after. "Right, right," I affirmed. "Raccoons are very smart. But what I'm wondering is, There's you, and Shoe, and a wild raccoon—in your car— driving to Thunder Lake Marsh. What I'm trying to figure out is, How did you all get to be in that situation?"

My mom considered my detective work with equanimity. She and Shoe had exchanged numbers after talking about water skiing. Mom had done a lot of skiing when she was Shoe's age, and she still did some tricking and slalomed whenever she could. One time Shoe called her—not to ski but because she had trapped a wild raccoon in her house. Now, I'm not exactly clear on the details of how the raccoon had come to live in her house or how she had acquired a trap, but neither of these facts was too far out of Northwoods normal. I had inferred that during the summer she lived with her dad. Sometimes her hair smelled of smoke from his cigarettes. He sounded like an old-timer for the region, so he probably had some traps around. Problem was, once Shoe had actually caught the raccoon, it—understand-ably—became unclear what the next move should be. Hence the late-night phone call. I hadn't really ever thought of my mother as the kind of person you'd call when being snarled at by an angry, trapped raccoon. But who *would* you call? Anyway, Shoe's intuition was right. Mom had an idea: Thunder Lake Marsh. It was a place she had heard of people discreetly discarding some expired gasoline.

Apparently, Shoe—the environmental science major—had been scandalized by that fact. My mom did an impression of her friend's learning about the old gas, shaking her fists at the sky in frustration: "Nooooooo!" It was as if imaginary Shoe were Darth Vader, having just discovered the love of his life wouldn't be returning from the dead. But Shoe still needed help. Her qualms about transporting contraband to a nature preserve sufficiently expressed, she acceded to the raccoon relocation plan. They were on the road to Thunder Lake Marsh.

"Sounds like Shoe really cares about marshland," I summarized.

"Well, what can you do with old gas?" Mom asked. "It'd cost a lot of money to take it to the dump!"

"You know who has a lot of money?" I countered. "Dave. Petronus."

"Pontilnic." Mom was neither amused nor annoyed. "We just didn't have a lot in common. He was a really nice guy."

"Did you ever see that raccoon again?"

"Never did."

And so it was that two lake girls, united by their peculiar history with the socially uncomfortable architect of a picture frame empire, defeated a wily rodent houseguest.[1]

"Nice work," I offered. Mom shrugged an acceptance.

Analysis

I've wondered about the story of Shoe and the wild raccoon. A better storyteller would leave its moral well enough alone. But this is not a story; it's a conceptual analysis.

This is an essay about being without guile. Remember that? Guile—or anyway the concept I have in mind, to which I'm attaching the word *guile* as a term of art—is not the same as deception. For one thing, guile is a feature of your character, or a kind of disposition with which you act generally. It's not a single instance of telling a lie or withholding a truth. More important, though, having guile need not involve deceiving anyone or trying to deceive anyone. Guile is just a way of deciding how to present yourself to others. Guile is the attitude you have when you see yourself, in your own mind's eye, from the other person's point of view and then decide how to act based on how you want *them* to see *you*.

That's a somewhat abstract way of putting a simple point. The waiter asks how you're doing, and you say, "Fantastic!" Neither of you takes this to be a genuine assertion about how you're

---

1. I'm told that my recollection of the story here bears a slight inaccuracy: the raccoon was not in the house but just on the premises.

doing. Maybe you're having a bad day and came to the Cheese-cake Factory for some caloric self-medication. But your waiter didn't need to know that and probably wouldn't want to. The waiter's query was really about whether your hamburger was cooked enough or if you wanted more ketchup. Your answer doesn't make you a liar, no matter that it was, strictly speaking, false. It was in no danger of deceiving anyone because both parties understood the pragmatic context of your utterance. You understood what your waiter was asking about, and you framed your answer so as to share a common aim that the question initiated. It's a kind of dance. A very simple one, but still a dance.

Guile need not even involve any semantic falsehoods. It can be revealed through our interpretive choices alone. The clerk at Men's Wearhouse asks me if I have any questions about their selection. Here are two entirely truthful answers: (1) Yes, I'm wondering if buying a suit in the current fashion would help me impress my prospective romantic partner from a higher social stratum? (2) Yeah, how much does this one cost? The clerk may well have useful opinions about both questions, but only one of these represents an effort to frame a reply with a conception of the clerk's intention already in mind. Answering in the first way reveals that I haven't understood how our interaction is mediated by the roles we inhabit—customer and salesperson. This is why we sometimes say that answers like the first "over-share" or violate a "boundary." These boundaries are the lines demarcated by the conventional social expectations of the roles we inhabit.

There's no deception in any of this. But ordinary choices in these settings reveal a kind of self-consciousness about how one presents oneself to others. My answer shows I've already thought about what the other person is expecting, and I respond in keeping with that customary social expectation. Before I know how to answer the question, I have to know the social context I'm in. Again, I'm not lying, but I am choosing which truths to tell.

This makes it sound like the issue is about authenticity. That's closer, but not quite right. Having guile doesn't make you inauthentic. Consider again the waiter at the Cheesecake Factory. Arguably, there's nothing inauthentic about acting like a waiter—being solicitous of customers' desires, appearing happy to accommodate requests, and the like. What would be inauthentic would be for the waiter to act like they were only a waiter, as if their intrinsic waiterliness guided every action they took as a person. This is what Sartre calls "bad faith." Here's his famous description of a waiter acting in bad faith:

> Let us consider this waiter in the cafe. His movement is quick and forward, a little too precise, a little too rapid. He comes toward the patrons with a step a little too quick. He bends forward a little too eagerly; his voice, his eyes express an interest a little too solicitous for the order of the customer. Finally there he returns, trying to imitate in his walk the inflexible stiffness of some kind of automaton while carrying his tray with a recklessness of a tight-rope walker by putting it in a perpetually unstable, perpetually broken equilibrium which he perpetually re-establishes by a light movement of the arm and hand.[2]

Lots of philosophers have thought that Sartre was onto something. There is a way of going wrong in life—of being inauthentic—that the waiter exhibits. The problem, it seems, is not

2. Jean-Paul Sartre, *Being and Nothingness*, trans. Hazel E. Barnes (London: Methuen and Co., 1969), 59. Quoted in D. Z. Phillips, "Bad Faith and Sartre's Waiter," *Philosophy* 56, no. 215 (January 1981): 23.

that he is acting like a waiter but that his performance is a little too thoroughgoing. As D. Z. Phillips pointed out, it's as though he's a "caricature of a waiter."[3] He is acting like he isn't acting at all, and that's what makes him an example of "bad faith."

Most people are not like this—at least most of the time. You can have guile without acting like you aren't acting. If you're like most people, there are different aspects to who you are, which together we might call your identity as a person. This is helpful, since these self-aspects can guide how we make choices in an automatic way. If you had to consciously think about your values and commitments every time you picked a conversation topic, planned an evening out, displayed an emotion to a loved one, and so on, life would quickly grind to a halt. There's too much going on in what we do, say, and feel to choose everything manually. Identities give us cognitive shortcuts. If I'm a birdwatcher and I hear a strange song in my yard, I'll go out to investigate. I won't pause to reconsider whether I should devote time to identifying different species. If you're my friend, you'll (I hope) pick up at least sometimes when I call. You won't reconsider whether it's worth your time before each conversation. Or, if you do, that might show our friendship is in trouble.

The different parts of our identity help us get through the day without overthinking everything all the time. These "self-aspects," as psychologists call them, aren't all active at once. If you're at home for Thanksgiving, you might represent yourself in one way. If you're at a meeting at work, you might act differently. My tennis-playing self talks to people differently than my philosophy self, and I try to keep both competitive and philosophical impulses under wraps during boring department meetings I'm compelled to sit through. There's nothing morally suspect about any of this. Nor is there anything inauthentic. It's

3. Phillips, "Bad Faith," 23.

not that I'm *really* a tennis fan who sometimes does philosophy. Your different self-aspects can all be a real part of you, in the sense that each expresses your actual values.

But things can get complicated. What happens when you can't neatly quarantine parts of your identity? In that condition, you might find there's no alternative besides manually deciding how to act, and that involves the kind of self-consciousness that can make things stressful. The philosopher Daniela Dover writes about the "acute discomfort" birthday parties sometimes present.[4] Suppose you're a fun-loving prankster around your siblings, introverted and cautious at work, and an occasionally irreverent baseball fan. Again, there's no reason to think there's anything inauthentic about this. There are just different parts of your identity that guide your actions in these varying settings. But now suppose people from those different parts of your life all show up to your birthday party. How should you act then? The issue is that the different parts of your identity might not all hang together at the same time. How much and how loudly will you talk? What will you say, or censor, or laugh at? The problem isn't that those in attendance won't get along with each other. The problem is that their presence will make potentially conflicting parts of your identity operative at once, and that will make for dilemmas in how to act. The problem, in other words, is that they might bring about a scenario in which you don't get along with yourself. That, according to Dover, is what makes birthday parties so stressful.

What I want to underscore is that if you suffer from this problem, that doesn't mean you're two-faced—at least not in the pejorative sense. Sure, you might wear different faces, but they could all be genuine. The problem is that the other-facing parts of you were chosen with respect to delimited groups of others,

4. Daniela Dover, "Identity and Influence," *Synthese* 202, no. 5 (2023): 17.

and it just so happened that those others brought out, called for, or otherwise made appropriate different personal traits. This is a roundabout way of saying that if you sometimes face the problem of birthday parties, it's because you have some guile. You choose whom to be a bit differently in different situations, with an eye toward getting along in the setting you happen to be in.

Contrast this with the person who has no guile. That person would not monitor their other-regarding actions with respect to different groups. They would try out the same jokes, no matter whether at work or home or the game. A lot of times, this makes things tougher. We might wince at how much they share with colleagues or furrow an eyebrow at how little they divulge to their loved ones. But it also comes with a benefit: they don't have to make any choices about which hat to wear on any given day. No one among their friends is perplexed at their behavior if they follow them into a different social environment. They don't have anything to fear about *choosing* whom to be at a birthday party. The guileless person and the guileful (?) person both live authentic lives. Neither represents themselves as having values which are actually not their own. But they live differently. One has different self-aspects that fit together across time but might not mesh together all at once. The other gets along with a streamlined self, forgoing ease of interaction in any given moment for a simplified global self-presentation.

Guilelessness as a Basis for Relationships
(Plus Some Thoughts about Jesus)

There's something to be said for an ideal of human relationships that prizes the unmediated self-presentation characteristic of guilelessness. However, the costs look steep. Guilelessness means forfeiting all the little things that can help you get ahead or get along. Saying the right thing to the right person at the right time. Making people feel good about themselves. Putting yourself in a position where other people want to do favors for you. None of that. To be without guile is to go without these gentle accoutrements.

Who could live like that? Well, Jesus. Think about the story of the "rich young ruler," first told in the Gospel of Mark.[5] Mark's Gospel is mostly the story of Jesus's journey, his being on "the way," eventually, to Jerusalem. "The way" refers not only to Jesus's itinerant journey but also to the divine presence that journey instantiated. "The way" is thereby also Mark's mysterious rendering of Jesus's announcement of the kingdom of heaven, which was somehow both imminent in Christ's promised return and already present in the supplicant's unqualified here-and-now commitment.

The young man finds Jesus on his journey. He's bursting with enthusiasm. He runs up to Jesus and asks what he must do to gain "eternal life" (Mark 10:17). Jesus answers by reciting the commandments as encoded in the Torah. Don't murder, don't commit adultery, etc. This is old news. "Teacher, I have kept all these since my youth," the young man says (10:21). Fair enough. He still lacks one thing, Jesus says: to give away all his money and follow Jesus on the way.

There are probably a hundred ways Jesus might have characterized God's kingdom to make it more appealing to an obviously well-heeled potential recruit. It's not that he wanted to get rid of the young man. Mark tells us that Jesus is genuinely impressed, even that he loves the young man. But he still matter-of-factly answers the young man's question in the most demor-

5. Mark doesn't actually call him this. That label is first applied later, in the Gospel of Matthew.

alizing way possible. The demand overwhelms the boy's former enthusiasm. He can't give up his many possessions, and goes away sad. Jesus then turns to his disciples to complain about rich people. "It is easier for a camel to go through the eye of a needle," Jesus says, "than for someone who is rich to enter the kingdom of God" (10:25). The disciples are shocked. Then it's impossible, they infer. And they would be right, except that doing the impossible is kind of God's thing. "For mortals it is impossible, but not for God; for God all things are possible" (10:27).

Peter can't help but notice that there are a few people around who have lived up to this demanding bit of instruction. "Look," he says, "we have left everything and followed you" (10:28). Maybe getting into heaven doesn't *always* take a miracle?

Peter really has given up everything. He is on the way with Jesus. It would be easy enough for Jesus to offer him just a little of the praise that he wants. Jesus will have none of it. You can imagine him rolling his eyes and cringing. His reply is comically sarcastic. Jesus agrees that those who have given up everything will get a fantastic return on their investment: "a hundredfold" of everything—"houses, brothers and sisters, mothers and children, . . . fields . . . persecutions" (10:30). His escalation gets increasingly absurd with each stop. You want a reward? Sure, Peter, you'll get a hundred times everything! A hundred houses! A hundred siblings! A hundred mothers! A hundred children! And a hundred persecutions.

Now, maybe you would want a hundred houses, and perhaps even a hundred brothers and sisters. But would you want a hundred children? A hundred mothers? That doesn't even make sense. The rejoinder ends on an even darker note. It looks for a moment like Jesus will pat Peter on the head, but at the last moment he twists the praise into an ominous rhetorical stomach punch.

Besides the (mostly affectionate) mocking, Jesus's point is typically elusive. Could it be something like this: that it's as much of a miracle for Peter to get into heaven as for the rich man, for whom it's just shy of metaphysically impossible? What's interesting is that for the second time in one conversation, Jesus has the chance to massage the truth a little, put a spin on it that acknowledges the point of view of the questioner. He ignores it. This is his standard mode of operating. As Josh Ritter points out in an album largely composed of unexpected biblical commentary, Jesus lives by the motto "When you get damned in the popular opinion, it's just another damn in the damns you're not givin'."[6] Jesus tells people the truth straight, even when he knows they will mishear it, take it the wrong way, use it against him, or whatever. He is the kind of being who could wear a facade but doesn't. When the social wheels could be greased with guile, he lets others be offended, chagrined, or downright bewildered. It makes it hard for some people to deal with him, even in the simplest of interactions. But it is also what makes him compelling.

This brings us back to Shoe, my mom, and the wild raccoon—but mostly to Shoe and my mom. I've never met Shoe, so my interpretation of this story will have to rely on a good dose of armchair speculation. I warned you this was a philosophy essay. My strong hunch is that Shoe and my mom came together not just by chance but also partly because they had something important in common. Mom wouldn't have talked to Shoe in her role as DNR boat-checker. She would have talked to her just as another person, without thinking about their social roles or places in life or any of the other euphemisms we deploy for politely skirting the humanity of others. Sometimes this can make things uncomfortable. But maybe Shoe was willing to listen to another person's unmediated particularity. Maybe she appreciated confronting another person not as the steward of a fairly boring job but just as another person. Maybe they started out

6. Josh Ritter, *Sermon on the Rocks*, Pytheas Recordings, 2015.

talking about personal things because, put in a position where they had to talk at all, that was—for them—the *only* thing to do. Maybe they didn't need to become friends, because talking in the way that friends do was how they talked all the time. (It is Wisconsin, after all.)[7] This is the beginning of trust. When someone lets you see them the same way they see themselves, then you get to know them. If they let you see everything about them, then it's easier to lower your emotional defenses. You don't have to worry about how they'll act in a new situation. The guileless person isn't keeping something back or managing their image. You can count on them to be who they are. In some sense, they don't have the option of being someone else.

Conclusion

St. Paul says we see through a glass darkly. He's right. For most of us, part of what it is to be a person obscures our self—at least our whole self, with all its multifaceted complexity—from the view of others. For that matter, if you think of Paul's translucent object as a looking glass—that is, a mirror—his point is deeper still.[8] Guile is, in the psychologist's parlance, how we operate on autopilot. It's so pervasive, and so effortless, that we may find it hard to tell when or whether we're acting at all. Agency's optics make for selves that are hard to see clearly, mirror or no. And as Paul likely intended, this includes one's own self perhaps most of all.

It won't always be this way. God knows us to our core, Paul thinks, and when Christ comes again, this knowledge will some-

---

7. This line was recommended to me by Jane Davis.
8. Probably Paul has in mind something like a polished, reflective piece of metal.

how be made public. In the eschaton—at the end of the world—we'll see face to face. In one great fell swoop, all those glassy objects distorting our view of ourselves will be gone. When the world is over, everything will be revealed. Maybe—with nothing left to conceal—we will finally be able to put guile to rest. If so, it's in good company. Paul says that all the virtues will be over with at that great and terrible day. Knowledge, wisdom, verbal dexterity, prophecy—all those traits you need to get ahead in this world of ours. They'll all be useless. All of them except one, that is. Love. Paul says that love is the only virtue that will still matter in a world where there's nothing left to hide.

The great Christian command is to love everyone. Treat everyone like your neighbor. It sounds impossible. There's a wide world out there, and we get precious little time in it. Loving relationships are intimate and difficult to maintain. How could we ever have them with everyone? It's tempting to think that Jesus must have meant something slightly different from what he said. Only, that's not really his thing.

In the long run, loving someone involves letting down our guard around them. You stop thinking about how to package what you say in order for it to make sense to the other person. You might even sometimes expect them to take in all the things you say without thinking at all and then make sense of it back to you—to help you make sense of yourself, to yourself. In the kingdoms of this world—a fallen world, to be sure—there aren't many people we allow ourselves to relate to in that way. But perhaps things could be different. The Gospel writers offer the example of Jesus as a kind of possibility proof. You don't have to be an omniscient, omnipresent, mysterious deity to abide the command to love all. You can do it while also being a flesh-and-blood human. If you are just enough without guile, you can end up on the way to Thunder Lake Marsh with anyone.

CHAPTER 6

The Dance

> I want to discuss some of the problems created by
> a disparity between the fragmentation of value and
> the singleness of decision. These problems emerge in
> the form of practical conflicts, and they usually have
> moral components.
>
> —Thomas Nagel, *Mortal Questions*

This is a story about fighting fish with a fly rod. It's also a story about how Nagel was right.

Background

The only stories in my family that gain immortality are those of lost fish. In the summer of 1995, I was creeping cautiously along the edges of a freestone stream in the northern part of Yellowstone National Park. The stream was Slough Creek, whose every section was the stuff of legend among fly anglers. Slough Creek flows from its headwaters high in the Beartooth Mountains down to the Lamar River. Along the twenty-five or so miles in between, it meanders lazily through four meadows. The upper three are known by fly-fishers as first, second, and third meadows. The lower meadow, somehow left out, was still home to a few Yellowstone cutthroat trout, as well as the occasional cutthroat-rainbow hybrid. I was alone—I think because my parents may have been upstream, in one of the stream's more famous meadows.

As a child, I was never more serious than when I was fly-fishing. I had literally read the book on Slough Creek the year before, completing a report on "Fly-fishing Yellowstone Waters" for my seventh-grade English glass. I now forget many of the details, but I remember the old, black-and-white photos accompanying each famous turn of the river, many named by fishers in the generation or two before my father started fishing that same country. The night before we left for "the park," excited and too nervous to sleep, I had reviewed an article from that summer's *In-Fisherman* magazine on how to play a hooked trout on a fly rod. Long before YouTube tutorials, and even before fly-fishing had been popularized enough to be the frequent subject of Saturday-morning fishing shows, I was content to review the detailed, step-by-step diagrams describing how to successfully fight a fish. Much as with learning to swing a tennis racquet or shoot a basketball, it's hard to learn how to move the rod just so by reading a book. But I was almost as serious about studying as I was about fly-fishing, so it seemed like the best option available.

By the time I reached Slough Creek's hallowed waters, I was prepared to treat each bend—every back eddy behind each overturned tree—with the greatest of caution. Without any bug life apparent, I found in my fly box an old attractor pattern—a Royal Coachman—in size 12. Today it would look like a fly from an old movie, but my teenage self was confident. In the mid-1990s, fly-fishing was dominated by tradition, not innovation, and it was still acceptable to use flies created by an earlier generation of fly tiers. The precursor of the Royal, the Coachman wet fly, was developed in the 1830s, outliving its namesake by nearly a century.

I crouched behind a few willows and tossed the fly gently into the center of a wide hole, watching it settle with a slight dimple on the calm surface. I glanced over the willows, careful that the fly should neither lag slower than the current nor push forward ahead of the stream's natural drift. It drifted carelessly atop Slough Creek's glassy surface. Nothing else was visible.

In an instant, a trout had shot out from an overhanging grassy bank to my right. It had crossed the width of the pool before I could begin to process its movement. It was on the fly, taking it, gliding back down into the invisible depths. My right hand, gripping tightly the cork handle of my Sage RPL+ rod, my only worldly possession of great value, was already moving sharply upward. The rod doubled over against the weight of the fish. Now the trout was jumping in the middle of the pool, nearly two feet above its surface. Its broad red stripe revealed it to be half-rainbow, the most acrobatic of Yellowstone's trout species. My eyes focused on its reentry into the water, but the trout was already on the far side of the pool. The line lagged, throwing a deep arc into the connection between rod and fish. The trout was jumping again on the far side of the pool, this time with leverage on its side. It cartwheeled in the air, putting pressure on the hook between the head of the fish and the line, still buried in the water. The fly popped out, and the fish slipped back into the water, leaving my rod lifeless in my hand. I could again hear the quiet gurgle of the stream from the head of the pool. A soft wind haunted the pines behind me. I stared at the clear pool, seeing straight to the bottom. It was empty, as if nothing had ever been there. Eventually, I became aware that the moment was over. How long had it been? Four seconds, maybe? Probably less.

June

I had wanted to fish with George since arriving as junior faculty at BYU. Years before, in grad school, Carey had given me George's book, *Home Waters*, which follows both a story and the descent of the Provo River from the High Uintas to its final destination at Utah Lake, just west of town. In the insert, Carey had written that it was a book about fly-fishing, Mormonism, and philosophy, and so—she reasoned—she had to give it to me as reassurance that *another* human held that configuration of interests. After settling into Provo life, I was delighted to find that the river was startlingly good fishing for a location just a fifteen-minute drive from my office. In the deep summer months, when light hangs in the canyon till ten at night, and caddis flies hatch for another half hour beyond that, you can get in a half day's fishing after a full day in the office. (You can also leave the office a bit early and reconfigure those ratios. Or so I've heard.)

Whenever I saw George around campus, I prodded him (gently) to come out to the river with me. He was busy with church, school, administration, the town, and family. "Keep after me," he would say. This last summer, with the last of his kids finally out of the house, he decided it was time to get back to fishing. This time, he said, he was really going to do it.

I have a running gimmick according to which I'm preparing for a backup career as a fly-fishing guide in the event that I'm denied tenure. This is mostly a joke, but I do like taking people out on the water. Taking someone fishing combines my two great interests, fly-fishing and devising strategy. What I've learned—very slowly—is that most people care more about something called "the experience" than they care about catching fish. I'm still not completely sure what the experience is, but it has something to do with sunsets and the smell of the pines and the evening light's glow on the water, its reflection distorted along the willows lining the bank. I don't fish for the experience. I fish for fish. Perhaps as an inheritance from my father, I would have thought that was the only way to do it. But along the way, having taken out many friends and colleagues, I've discovered that many people are really after the experience. As in all things, values are more diverse than you'd guess.

I say all this because, despite knowing most folks don't share my values, I can't bring myself to invite someone fishing until I've figured out how to do it in a way that will get them to succeed by *my* lights—by the metric of catching fish. By the middle of June, I was confident. I had fished around the perimeter of Strawberry Reservoir, Utah's premier fly-fishing destination, finally locating large schools of native Bonneville cutthroat trout. Named after the state's prehistoric inland sea, the Bonneville cuts evolved, unlike other trout, to eat small fish in open water. If you can find them just before dusk on a summer evening, they will likely be on the move and searching for prey. And in the middle of June, I knew where they were. The week before, I had hooked some twenty trout in a quiet back bay, where they roamed the shallows at sundown. I called George to tell him the time had come.

We picked up Terryl on our way to the lake. Terryl had been wanting to get into fly-fishing and had purchased his own rod and vest. I don't know if I've ever come across a subject in which Terryl was not curious. He agreed to come without hesitation. I started telling him the details of how we would catch fish, and he waved me off over the phone. "We'll do whatever you say," he said.

My dad says that nothing in the out-of-doors goes exactly to plan. I had been watching the weather for favorable conditions, looking for a calm night with a slight offshore wind. On the way to the lake, however, a dark thunderhead hovered right over Strawberry Valley. Just as we arrived at my starting location, the summer storm unleashed its mix of wind, rain, and hail on the lake. I hoped that George and Terryl would want to wait it out. We had only a few hours before sundown, and we would have a hard time getting out to the fish in float tubes without using all those few precious hours. They offered a modification on my plan: drive back to the lodge, get something for dinner, and then come back to the lake again after eating.

The summer shower over and dinner complete, we got back to the lake with the golden light of sunset already inching toward the water. As I set up the float tubes on the shore of the bay, Terryl encountered a few kids fishing for crawdads with chicken legs. He inquired about how it worked, showing considerable acuity, and his small but friendly interlocutors happily obliged. I think he would have been just as interested in the pursuit of crawdads as trout.

By the time I got out to the water, George had already caught a healthy, 18-inch cutthroat. I passed him, admiring it in his net, and kicked my way out to Terryl, who had never fished from a float tube. It can take some getting used to. There's a reason most people associate tubes with reclining peacefully in a pool rather than actively casting on a windswept reservoir. Approaching Terryl, I took the liberty of offering an overview of the strategy: Proceed along the shoreline's outer perimeter, keeping the fly in the lake's littoral zone, where shallow water breaks to deeper depths. Look for current seams created by the evening wind as it blows water across emergent vegetation. Keep the fly moving; without any disturbance on the surface of the water, it won't be visible enough to attract large trout from deeper water. I had tied on various terrestrial patterns, as early summer fish were still willing to rise from midrange depths to take surface flies, especially as shadows grew in the evening.

Nothing in fishing is that complicated, though we sometimes like to explain it as if it were. I suspect we do this to maintain the veneer of intellectual cachet that fly-fishers somehow enjoy. All the same, hooking a fish with a fly rod can be a bit tricky. Seeing a fish take your small ant pattern nearly eighty feet away, in uneven water and fading light, and then timing the hookset to drive a point measuring about 1/32 of an inch into a rising fish just as it turns back toward the depths (and not a moment sooner)—all of this takes a bit of feel beyond the range of linguistic articulation. Doing all of this with a nine-foot fly rod, with its soft tip slowing the response time between the movement of one's arm and the hook's response, makes everything harder still.

The postprandial fishing was going slower than I had hoped, but it was not long before a trout surfaced, engulfing Terryl's fly. In a moment it was gone, the distance between rod and fly making a solid hookset difficult. A few other fish likewise eluded capture, with one thing or another going amiss. A few minutes later, rounding a secondary point in our cove, another cutthroat came up, took the fly, and submerged. This one held on a moment longer, Terryl's rod doubling over with the weight of the fish. Perhaps not quite aware it had been hooked, the large trout moved toward us, and the line went slack. Sensing the urgency of the moment, I gestured emphatically for Terryl to catch up to the approaching fish.

"Reel! Reel! Reel!" I yelled at a volume exceeding what our proximity demanded. Terryl started winding the line in, taking in several yards of slack line. "I think the fish might be gone," he observed.

"Keep reeling! Keep reeling!" I grabbed the line below his rod's final eyelet, hauling it in with my free hand. The trout turned and descended to the depths. I saw the line running back out and exhaled in relief. The line was taut again, the rod again bent toward the fish, its tip vibrating with life. Terryl was still reeling, even as the fish opposed the tight line. There was no hint it was tired. The bend in the rod deepened dangerously. I imagined the 5X tippet—the thinnest bit of line used to secure the fly—must be nearing its breakpoint.

"Stop . . . Stop! Stop!" I heard myself pleading. "Stop!"

Terryl methodically removed his hand from the reel. "I'm just trying to follow your instructions," he replied, reasonably. At that, rod released like a bow, line shooting out back toward the fish. The line was slack again.

I reacted to the newly revised situation. "Reel! Reel! Reel! Reel!"

Terryl looked at me over the top of his sunglasses. "You're sure?" he asked, wryly.

"Everything I say makes sense in the moment I say it!" I was half-apologetic, but my eye was on the pile of line that needed to be taken in. Through it all, the trout somehow stayed attached, and after repeating my urgent demands a few more times as the fish dived, retreated, and dived again, I plunged my net into the dark water and emerged with a Bonneville cutthroat trout. I could hardly contain my excitement. "What a fish!" I cried. Terryl observed it impassively.

"Well, I can tell Fiona we weren't skunked," he observed. He looked it over again. Somehow, for him, the reality fell shy of the hype. "It seemed like it would be bigger."

◆ ◆ ◆

Night comes late to the mountains in June. A few more chances had slipped through our fingers, and we finished out the night without any more fish. By the time we were on our way back to Heber, it was after ten. George was talking about how he had fallen in love with fly-fishing after moving to Utah as a young literature professor. "I thought about it all the time," he said. "I even had dreams in which I was fly-fishing." He talked about how excited he was to find any space of time to get out on the river. "My heart would start beating out of my chest," he explained. "It felt as if I were cheating on my wife."

"With fly-fishing?" I asked, trying for a joke.

"It felt just the same as when I was falling in love," he replied, treating the question earnestly.

"If love of fishing counts as betrayal, I've never been faithful to anyone," I said.

I could not very well imagine George cheating on his wife, but I doubt that he has much of an idea of what that would be like, either. "Well, OK," he acknowledged. "It just felt like a kind of relationship."

Like a relationship. In a moment, the topic pivoted to how George fell in love with Amy at first sight upon meeting her at Stanford. That's a longer story, but by its end I had serious doubts that any impurity had ever really intruded on George's heart. The conversation drifted from there to some of George's work for the city and then to various complaints about Utah politics. Then I heard Terryl's voice again, startling me with his sudden reentry.

"I've had to repent many times for wanting things to be better," he said, from the darkness of the back seat. Even the church—to which both Terryl and George were deeply dedicated—had its imperfections. But it struck me as something approaching a conceptual truth that it would be good for things to be better. Wanting things to be better hardly seems like the sort of desire for which one would need to repent.

I turned around and glanced at him over my shoulder. Though always seeing the best in the people around him, Terryl was given to a feeling of dissatisfaction with things, but I wouldn't have described it as a vice, let alone a sin. Seeing my question, he said, "It's good that the world disappoints us."

"Why do you say this?" I asked out loud.

Terryl enjoys a challenge, taking it as a mark of friendship or respect or maybe both. He answered in a way that gave me the idea he had been preparing for the question. "It frustrates our terrestrial ambition that status should track worthiness. The thought that we should get recognition in this world is something to overcome."

"OK," I nodded.

The Dance: Lesson 1

"Are you in Provo?" Laurie texted me. I had known Laurie since she was maybe eleven years old, but we hadn't really been friends until sitting outside during the dancing portion of Carey's wedding. A year or two after that, she had started college at BYU. When she was in town during the summer, she was occasionally interested in going fly-fishing on the lower Provo River. Or, rather, she was interested in the local curiosity of fly-fishing on the lower Provo River. I replied that I was in my office, as usual. "Want to go fishing?" she wrote.

Laurie was on a quick getaway from her DC government job. I met her at the park, and we were on our way to the river for the last couple of hours before dark. This time, I told her, we were timing things just right. By the middle of July, the caddis hatch had started on the Provo, the most important fishing event of the year in Utah County. The key was to find the water that fish would move into right before dark. In the few places where the river's wild brown trout would concentrate to feed on the hatching flies, you could have a take on almost every cast for the magical fifteen minutes separating late dusk from complete darkness.

Laurie stared out the passenger window, content enough to take in the summer evening as we drove up Provo Canyon.

Chapter 6

Leaving the parking spot, we walked down to the river and along the old railroad track, scouting for a place to fish. It's a delicate business. At the height of the caddis hatch, there are more fishers than locations where fish will feed, a fact which is itself a matter of public knowledge. But on this night, something extraordinary happened. Someone got out of the water on the most productive bend of the entire river just as we walked by. Seeing him get up to the bank behind us, I hurried us back, almost frantic. We descended the steep shoreline to the sharp curve in the river. The main current hit the end of the channel, doubling back in two side currents flowing upstream for ten or twelve yards. One of those currents cut back along the shoreline; the other formed a seam with the main river, creating a narrow band where the eddy brushed against the main current. Between them, a gravel bar rose nearly to the surface, creating a further break in the current for nearly thirty yards. All of these current edges on one feature of the river create an ideal location for the fish to feed. A trout could sit comfortably in the calm water behind the bar as bugs drift by on the surface and then swirl back again in the eddy. So many caddis would end up caught between the two currents that any artificial fly sitting among them would catch on to several emerging bugs.

Easing our way into the river, I was triumphant at our luck. "We command the best water from the High Uintas to Utah Lake!" I gestured grandiosely, sweeping the tip of my Sage rod from the mountains I imagined to our northeast to the lake fifteen miles below us.

Laurie shrugged. "So, we're gonna give it a try here, are we?" she asked, smiling.

We set up on the tip of the long gravel bar, facing downstream. I pointed to both lines of current. Once we start seeing caddis in the air, I told her, that was the moment. We had to keep the flies in the water directly below us. She threw her line downstream, pulling out sections to let the caddis imitation drift downstream below her—five feet, then ten, then twelve. You want the fly to linger in the space between the currents. The water is uneven but slow moving. That's why the fish are there.

The tip of Laurie's rod flickered. "What?" she said, puzzled. (Our prior outings didn't have the greatest track record for actual fishing success.)

"You have one!" I declared. "You have one!"

"What now?" she asked.

"Rod tip high!" I barked. She glanced my way quizzically, then again at her line. She looked at the sleek blue graphite pole in her hand as if to regret that she and the trout on the other end had gotten themselves into this predicament. The line was slack, and, in a moment, the trout was off.

"Is that fish still out there?" she asked, moving the lifeless rod up and down.

"Oh, he's still out there," I answered, "but not at the end of your line." Laurie smiled brightly.

"Too bad!" she said.

"When you hook a fish," I went on, undeterred, "you want to keep the line tight. Once the line is slack, there's nothing holding the point of the hook in the fish's mouth."

"Hmm." Laurie nodded.

She threw the line downstream again, repeating the drift along the current break behind the bar. And again—almost in an instant—a fish was on, I was laughing with excitement, and Laurie was obligingly holding the line tight in her left hand. This time the brown slipped into the deep side of the bar and started downstream with the main current of the river. The end of the line shot downstream.

"You have a good one!" I cried. Laurie glanced back toward me from her rod.

Chapter 6

"Are you so happy now?" she asked, hopefully.

"I am so happy now!" I was about a third of the way through that sentence when the trout hit the end of fly line sitting on the water and the rod loaded fully against the combined weight of the fish and the current. The 5X tippet connecting the dry caddis to the smaller, trailing fly behind it snapped in protest.

"That was fast!" Laurie declared.

This was the moment I had been waiting for.

"So," I began, "I've been working on a lecture about how to land a fish with a fly rod. Would you mind if, for my own benefit, I try it out on you?"

"Absolutely!" Laurie held on to each syllable (*ab-so-lute-ly*), inflecting her voice with a musical cadence. What Laurie lacked in interest in fly-fishing she made up for with delight in absurd spectacle. "I will gladly listen to your lecture."

I started in. When you are in the business of giving lectures for university general education requirements, you take any spark of excitement a fellow human will offer. "So, the thesis is that playing a large fish is like a dance. You want to keep firm contact with the fish, but just enough to guide it. You don't want to pull it around. You want your movements to be in time with the fish's movements."

"Hold on," Laurie said. "You know how to dance?"

"Oh, no," I said. "I'm just interested in the concept."

"Of . . . dancing?"

"Well, there's a part of *A River Runs through It* that describes fighting a large fish as a dance between the angler and the trout."

"Wait," Laurie stopped again. "You've read *A River Runs through It*?"

"Oh no, of course not."

"Saw the movie?"

"Ehh, no."

"Never mind." Laurie waved her hand as if to dismiss her entire line of questioning. "Go on," she encouraged.

"Toward the end of the book," I said, "there's several pages just dedicated to explaining in detail how one of the characters plays a big fish . . ." Laurie raised an eyebrow at my renewed summarizing. "Jess sent me text messages with pictures of the relevant pages," I explained. "I actually read them a few summers ago standing in this very spot, waiting for the caddis hatch."

"So, the character is fighting a fish?" Laurie directed.

"He's fighting a fish," I agreed. "And the idea is that it's like a dance. When you're dancing with someone, you don't want your limbs to be slack, because apparently—I think—that doesn't adequately signal to your partner which way you're moving. On the other hand, you don't want to move against your partner too sharply, because that will push them or pull them off course. So, the guiding idea," I said, clasping one of my hands with the other and moving them back and forth together as if my two arms connected respective dancing partners, "is to always maintain a firm pressure on each other's hands, but not so much pressure that you get off balance. You want just enough resistance to move together."

Laurie frowned. "This isn't working for me."

"This is the first time I've ever given this lecture."

"When you're dancing, the man is the one who leads," she said. "And our point in fishing is to catch the fish. So, we're like the man in the story, and the fish is like the woman. That makes it seem like the woman is an object of pursuit and capture."

I frowned. "I see what you're saying," I admitted. "I'm not endorsing . . ."

"Oh, I know," Laurie said.

"Let me try to think through this." I took off my hat and ran my fingers through my hair. "I'm not saying that catching a fish is a metaphor for dancing. I'm just saying that dancing is a metaphor for catching a fish."

"I don't like it," she insisted.

"I didn't write the book."

"You didn't read the book."

"Look," I said, "I'm just trying to get you to reel when the fish is coming toward you and let the line go when the fish is going away from you."

"You're gonna need a new metaphor," Laurie observed.

The Dance: Lesson 2

The caddis hatch is the river's highest drama. Shadows lengthen across the stream. The cool evening breeze blows down the canyon. A moment arrives when, in the reflected final light of dusk, the whole valley glows golden yellow. Warblers in the trees sing with the urgency of mountain summer's last light. Still, nothing. I've watched countless fly-fishers give up and, discouraged, leave the best runs on the river. Every year—literally every year—there are days in the early summer when I look around to the few anglers who share their secrets and their water with me, and I say, "I'm not sure it's going to happen." The caddis hatch will try your faith. You know the script; you've rehearsed so many times. And yet, it takes longer than you remember, longer than it seems like it possibly could. Only at the last moment, the moment when your doubt is real, the last possible moment—only then. The caddis appear as if from nowhere. And in a moment, they're everywhere—on the water, swirling around the air, crawling on your clothes and face. That's the moment when it happens.

It was on one of these nights, deeper in July, when I met Dave and a work colleague of his on the river. We had a tradition—

going back to graduate school—of spending a summer evening fishing or throwing a baseball for a while and then finding our way to a nearby McDonald's. Dr. Ian was new to fly-fishing, so I had the chance to go through my usual spiel about the shape of the river. We were at the opening of a deep pool, a place where the river opens up after a narrow run and extends in a long tail out, finally turning into a riffle some seventy yards below us. At this opening, the current forms a back eddy. The current from the eddy runs back along the shoreline and up into where the rapids upstream empty into the pool. The result is another crease of "soft water," a place where two opposing currents run into each other, forming a line some ten yards long at the top of the pool. I stood next to Dr. Ian, running the tip of my rod along the imaginary line where the current from the eddy folded back into the main river.

"There!" I said. "That's where you want your fly."

The drama of the evening concluded, as it sometimes but not always does, with the arrival of the caddis. They were everywhere. Dr. Ian hooked a good brown trout, and the fish retreated into the deep water in the center of the run. The trout's retreat put pressure on the rod, which was now nearly horizontal to the water. In a second or two, the trout was off.

"Huh," Dr. Ian said, looking down the rod at the empty water.

"Dr. Ian, would you mind if I offer some advice about the fly rod?" I asked.

"Please," he replied, congenially.

"You want to keep the tip of the rod up. That way, the fish pulls against the whole rod, and the soft tip of the rod keeps the line tight when the fish moves toward you and absorbs the pressure when the fish turns and runs the other way." I swung the tippet into my left hand and pulled, drawing the rod tight like a bow to illustrate. "See, I can pull the line and let it out again and the deep bend in the rod keeps the line tight but not too tight."

The hatch was still on, and in a moment the fish was running with the current, Dr. Ian's line shooting through the guides of the rod till it reached the end and the fish connected directly with the fly reel. Dr. Ian held the reel firmly in his hand. As the trout hit the end of the line with the current at its back, the fly popped immediately under the pressure.

"This isn't easy," Dr. Ian noted.

My moment had arrived. "Could I interest you in a lecture on playing a trout with a fly rod?" My voice was obviously hopeful.

Accustomed to academic lecture giving, Dr. Ian was gracious. "I would like that," he said.

"It's called the Dance," I said. And I laid out for him the central points, especially the importance of keeping pressure on the fish—just enough to keep the line tight but not so much that the line might break. I pointed at the calm water in the eddy to our right. "You want to use the length of your rod to guide the fish," I said. "Every time you have a chance to put pressure on the fish, maneuver him toward the calm water. Out there"—I pointed to the churning water in the river's main current—"all is lost if a big trout gets into that stuff." I modeled with my own rod, swooping it broadly down and away from us. "You don't just want to hold the rod at the same angle all the time; think about where you want the fish to be. That way you can keep the fight from getting away from you in the heavy current." Dr. Ian nodded. "But if the fish makes another run, then take your hand off the reel and move the rod back toward the fish. Just like in a dance, your actions are so closely coordinated with what the fish is doing that if someone were watching from the outside, it would look just like you were acting together."

"This is a helpful lecture," Dr. Ian graciously offered.

"It's a work in progress."

"It's informative!"

"Some people tell me that it's sexist," I said.

We caught a few more fish and made our way up the old railroad trail to our cars. You could barely see your way forward in the scattered reflection of final light, but the first stars were making their way out above the Wasatch.

"Who says your lecture is sexist?" Dave asked.

"Laurie."

"Hmm." Dave nodded as if to mull over the accusation. "Because you're trying to catch the fish?"

"That's right. She says I need a different metaphor."

"You could say it's like walking a dog," Dave suggested.

"Is that better?"

"Maybe it's like flying a kite?"

"These are good suggestions," I said, mustering a supportive tone. Dave shrugged. We had reached our cars.

"So," he asked, "McDonald's?"

The Dance: Lesson 3

"Let's go fish," George texted me. We were off to the Provo once again. The caddis hatch lingers into August, and the prospect for good fishing along with it. We waited. The shadows lengthened along the canyon. We waited some more.

"I think it might be over," George suggested.

"The caddis hatch tries our faith."

When it might have seemed like darkness was already upon us, the fish started rising along the soft water between the currents. I glanced to the tail of the pool, and George had hooked a fish. His vintage Sage four-weight convulsed with the unseen trout's headshakes. George stepped a foot or two deeper into the pool as the fish dived. His line slackened. It was as if life had gone out of the rod. He glanced my way. "I think he has me in a log down there," he said, pulling his rod at different angles to undo the snag. "What do you suppose happened?" George wondered. Never one to turn down the chance to do a postgame analysis of a moment of fly-fishing, I rehearsed my views about anticipating better and worse places to fight the fish.

"You want to anticipate where in the river it would be better to fight the fish. Guide the fish that way. Put pressure on the fish to use energy in a place where he can't do as much damage to you. If you let the fish dive to the bottom, bad things will happen. You have to turn the fish before he gets there." My advice sounded good to me as I was saying it.

Seconds are precious in the flurry of caddis flies. In another moment, George was hooked up again, this time on a longer cast out into the river's central current. The fish turned downstream, catching the current like a sail in the wind. George held his position and moved his rod so as to swing the fish's head back upstream. His rod doubled as it pulled against the fish and the current, and the 5X tippet connecting him to the fish gave way.

"Sorry!" I yelled over the sound of the river. "There was too much current out there to get him back into the calm water."

"I guess I should've tried to follow him," George mused.

"Good idea!" I declared. "*The fish has to lead.*" George was back to casting in the last rays of light. "Playing the fish is like a dance. You want your rod's movement above the water and the trout's moves beneath to so seamlessly intertwine that when viewed from the outside, it would be as if it were one motion jointly enacted. But when the trout takes off downstream, you have to do your best to follow suit. In a dance choreographed by the river's current, you have to let the fish lead."

I was talking to myself. But, as I say, for a gen ed teacher, that's nothing to worry about. Next time, I told myself, I would have the right words.

Darkness came next, as it always does, and we walked back up the train tracks. George loved the river too much to be discouraged. But he also loved fly-fishing enough to practice the rite of considering the one that got away. "I wonder what I could have done differently," he mused.

I nodded my sympathy. What I said was, "Sometimes there's nothing you can do." But what I wish I had said was, "It's good the river disappoints us." Maybe next time.

The Thing They Don't Tell You

The clock on the conference room wall showed 4:01. "It takes a few minutes for everybody to filter in," I said, as if to apologize. Even as I said it, I was aware that none of the TAs already there minded starting the meeting late.

"It's getting to be that time of the semester," Luke said.

"Did you and your wife end up going camping over the weekend?" I asked him.

"Yeah," he said, bleakly.

"At the end of the day, it's just sleeping on the ground," I replied.

"That's exactly what happens at the end of the day," he nodded. "Plus, it took the whole weekend. Now I feel like I'm way behind on a bunch of projects."

Brad moved forward in his chair, as if prompted by a thought. We all looked at him. "Well," he said, "if you had stayed home to work, do you think you would have regretted missing the trip?"

Luke mulled over the question. "Yeah. Maybe so. But as it is, I still regret it!"

The door was opening behind us as Jamie and Adrienne slipped into the room.

"Regret what?" Jamie asked.

"Luke and his wife went camping, and now he regrets it, but we're telling him he shouldn't," I summarized.

"You were not there," Luke said.

"Oh, I wasn't making a point about camping," I said. "Just the concept of regret. Regret has two appropriateness conditions: first, that you made a bad choice; second, that if you had made the other choice, things would have gone better."[1]

"Why does it follow he shouldn't regret going camping?" Jamie asked, curious. She turned to Luke. "I just want you to feel good about feeling bad about your terrible choices," she consoled.

"Thanks for that," Luke said. Jamie nodded obligingly.

The stakes were getting a little higher, but I felt like I was still on solid ground. "Regret implies you ought to have made a different choice. If something bad would've happened either way, the fact that something bad happened in the real world doesn't tell in favor of the alternative. It's disappointing but not a cause for regret. Sometimes the world just gives you a bad hand."

"I regret starting this conversation," Jamie offered.

"Excellent case," I affirmed.

"But I can't regret going camping?" Luke asked.

"Jamie was in a position to know better."

"Couldn't I have been in a situation where I would've regretted whichever thing I did?" Luke maintained.

Brad moved as if to reenter the conversation. We looked his way. "Well . . ." he said, "my feeling is that for some actions, it doesn't make sense to regret taking it if you know you also would have regretted not taking it."

1. Dan Moller, "Anticipated Emotions and Emotional Valence," *Philosopher's Imprint* 11, no. 9 (July 2011): 1–16, https://tinyurl.com/hjyh6nyv; see also R. Jay Wallace, *The View from Here: On Affirmation, Attachment, and the Limits of Regret* (Oxford: Oxford University Press, 2013).

"I'm on Brad's side," I said, pointing a finger at him. He looked ambivalent.

"I'm not sure," Jamie said.

"I think it's time ... we could—if we want to—start the meeting," Adrienne offered. She had taken a stack of exams out of her bag and was organizing them on the table in front of her.

"And we will!" Luke affirmed, nodding in the clock's direction. "Real quick, though: what's the case that regret is incompatible with regretting the counterfactual?"

"Have I talked to y'all about *La La Land*?" I asked.

"You absolutely have talked about that, yes," Luke replied.

I was not deterred. "You've all seen it?" I asked.

Luke and Brad nodded. "Yep," Jamie replied.

"I actually never saw it," Adrienne interjected again from the far side of the table.

Jamie looked at her. "Movie night?" Adrienne returned her glance with the slightest apprehension, her eyes flickering to the exams on the table in front of her.

"Alright," I said, gesturing as if I was going to give the story as compactly as possible. Then I glanced to Adrienne. "You mind some mild spoilers?"

She looked resigned. "Maybe this will motivate me to watch it."

"OK," I said. "Emma Stone and Ryan Gosling break up, and years later she and her husband show up at Ryan Gosling's jazz bar. She sees him there, he starts playing the piano, and then all of a sudden they're back to where they first met, and the movie reimagines everything happening differently. It goes through the whole counterfactual. They don't argue; instead, they kiss. They work things out rather than fight. He doesn't miss her show. She becomes a star. He follows her to Paris. Everything is different, and they end up together. Then the counterfactual version of the story catches up to where they are in the present, only this time it's Emma Stone and Ryan Gosling sitting together, listening to the piano. At the end, the camera pans around the bar to Emma Stone's face—and she's so happy!"

"So far this is literally just a description of the movie," Luke observed.

"I'm trying to help you not feel irrationally bad about your life."

"Go on," he encouraged.

I leaned across the table to underscore my point. "The important thing is that even though we've now seen how everything could have gone differently, *we don't yet know whether it's a cause for her to regret her real-world choices*. Because, for all we know, she might also be so happy in the real world too, the world where she marries someone else. The movie takes us back to real life, where she and her real-life husband are watching Ryan Gosling play the song. And as his song ends, the camera pans back around the bar." I pause for effect, as if panning an imaginary camera around the classroom, looking for Emma Stone's face.

"And everyone is wondering, How will Emma Stone look?" I keep up my imaginary panning. "What expression will be on her face?"

"I don't know if I even remember," Jamie said.

"I'm going to tell you," I reply. "The camera gets to her face." I stop panning as if Jamie is Emma Stone.

"She isn't happy. *She is not happy*. That's why the ending is devasting. She is happy in the counterfactual world when the piano stops playing, but in the real world she isn't. The choices *did* matter. It's a case of real regret."

"I don't remember feeling that sad at the end," Luke said.

"I felt a little sad," Jamie mused.

Brad moved from side to side in his chair. "I'm not sure."

I waved my hand as if to dismiss all of them. "I don't know why I get so much resistance to my obviously correct interpretation!"

"You . . . argue about the meaning of *La La Land* frequently?" Jamie asked.

I shook my head in frustration. "Jessica Flanigan says I don't understand the meaning of my own favorite movie."

"Why does she say that?" Adrienne asked. We all looked at her. She nodded as if to affirm her continued presence in the room.

"She says you're meant to think that Emma Stone made the right choice by breaking up with Ryan Gosling, even though there was something sad about it."

"Perhaps as if she could regret either thing . . ." Luke observed wryly.

"Tell me the case for her side," Jamie asked.

"The case for her side is that the movie gives clues to show that Emma Stone is a bigger star in the real world where she and Ryan Gosling break up. She has a bigger house, a nicer car. She's on the billboards. Remember the song she sings about the fools who dream? There are pros and cons, but the movie is on the side of following dreams and breaking hearts and making a mess."

"Hmm . . ." Jamie mused. "What's your response to that response?"

Adrienne exhaled softly.

"I agree the movie is on the side of following your dream and making a mess," I said. "But there's a question what to do once you've decided you're the dreamer. The dream was never about the house or the car or the billboard. It was about a future where Emma Stone is really happy."

Jamie looked dubious. "Yikes, Dr. Davis. I feel like Jessica Flanigan has a pretty good case."

"I'm still not sure," Brad said.

"We might just have to watch the movie again," Jamie suggested, her inflection upward, as if posing a question, with an encouraging nod to Adrienne.

"OK," Luke declared. "Time for grading?" He was taking a stack of exams out of his own bag.

"Wait. Everybody sign this," Jamie said, handing Luke a manilla placard.

"What is that?" I asked.

1

The clock in the back of the auditorium read 10:02. "Alright," I said, mustering a loud voice to start class. This is your final warning. Only twenty-four hours separate you from the midterm exam."

An audible groan went up from the class. "I know," I said. "Exams are terrible."

Someone in the back of the room sighed. "Then why do we have them?"

"There's no good answer to that question," I admitted. "It's a bad system, and it makes no sense. I'm sorry."

"Is that . . . the real answer?" someone asked.

"It is."

"Then why do we have to take the test?" another student chimed in.

"We live in a fallen world," I replied. A pair of students on the second row rolled their eyes.

"Wait, are you not sure if I'm joking?" One student shrugged, and the other nodded.

I turned my attention back to the whole class. "Nobody actually thinks that exams are good, do they? Anybody who likes exams, raise your hand now!"

I had taken myself to be joking, but a smattering of students hesitantly raised their hands.

"Good, good," I said. "I respect the courage it takes to support such an obviously false view."

A student near the back raised her hand, and I nodded to her. "Well," she began, "if we didn't have exams, then I wouldn't be motivated to do the reading."

"And you want to have to do things you don't feel motivated to do?"

"Well," she said again, "sometimes I just need something to motivate me to do what I want to do."

"Is reading for this class one of those things?" I asked her.

"I think it might be," she said.

"You want to read Hobbes?"

"Well . . ." she frowned.

Another student interjected, "The problem with exams is it makes everything too stressful."

"I'm glad someone is on my side," I said.

The student went on: "It just makes it seem like not everyone can succeed. Like some people have to do worse than others."

I nodded emphatically. "The grading curve is the great enemy of Zion!" A few students made a sound halfway between a laugh and groan.

"I'm serious!" I said. "What's the opposite of Zion?" I didn't wait for anyone to answer. "It's when people are divided by their status and chances for learning. Zion is when people are unified, and the grading curve is for people to be distinguished. The Book of Mormon literally says that—I guess except for the part about the curve."[2]

No one said anything for a moment, and we all stared at each other.

"Anyway," I said, "it feels bad to feel like you're worse than other people."

There was another pause, and then a student raised his hand. "Yeah, but does that happen *to you*?" he asked.

2. 3 Nephi 6:12.

I nodded gravely. "When I was in grad school, I heard about this guy over in England. Rumor was he was going to be the greatest Kant scholar in the world. At first I felt a little twinge of jealousy, but then I learned he had corrected the translation of some famous passage from the original German."

"He might not be that great," the student encouraged.

"Yeah, that's what I thought," I affirmed. "But then I met him, and it took me about thirty seconds to realize I would never catch up to him in logic."

"What's this guy's name?" the student wondered.

"How did we get on to talking about me?" I wondered.

"Just tell us his name!"

"Simon."[3]

Another student intervened. "Maybe Simon is just so into philosophy, he has no life at all!"

"You know, I hoped for that," I said. "But then it turned out he was also excellent at extreme sports. He's a semiprofessional boxer, or something like that."

"I bet he has no friends," the student countered, hopefully.

"Yep, I tried that too," I said. "But then it turned out he had a beautiful and happy marriage."

"Simon is terrible!" the first student declared.

"And the worst part," I continued, "is that you can't even resent him for it. He's actually been really helpful to me in my career, to no benefit at all for himself."

The second student shook her head in disgust. "Simon *is* the worst!" she piled on.

"Thank you," I said.

The first student shook his fist in outrage. "Down with Simon!"

---

3. I've changed the name, although I feel like "Simon" looks pretty good in this story.

"We hate that guy!" someone called out from the back of the room. A round of scattered applause went up in support of opposition to Simon's excessive virtues.

The moment passed, and insults against a guileless philosopher somewhere in England began to subside.

"Well, anyway," I said, "the exam is tomorrow."

2

"Come in," I said in a loud voice, turning around from my desk. There were no assignments imminently due, so it was a little surprising to have customers during office hours. A student slipped through the door and dropped her backpack next to my office chair.

"Hi Rozlyn!" I said.

"I just wanted to ask about some of the readings for this week," she replied. "I came by before class, but you weren't here."

"Oh, I teach another section right before our class," I said.

"Another section of 202?" she asked. I nodded. She proceeded to offer some notably detailed questions about Locke's *Second Treatise on Government*. She had some complaints about Locke's reasoning. Once satisfied that she had presented her objections, Rozlyn got up to leave.

"By the way," I said, "I liked your questions to Ambassador Flake the other day. I didn't know you were a debater."

"Yeah, I debated in high school," she replied. She then paused a moment. "I didn't remember I told you that."

"You didn't," I said. "But you numbered the points in your question, and also you used your debate voice to ask it."

"Debate voice?" she inquired.

"Don't you think?"

"I suppose I did change my voice a little when I was a debater."

"Everybody does," I said. "That's what they teach you to do in the 'perceptual dominance' lab at camp."

"You've been to debate camp?" she asked.

"I taught at debate camp up till I took this very job," I said, gesturing to my office.

"I thought about debating again, but I decided to get out of it," she reported.

"Good for you," I told her. "Get out while you still can!" She laughed slightly.

"It takes all your time," she agreed. "I was the president of my debate team in high school." I nodded. "You know," she said, "I actually checked when I arrived at BYU and saw you were the advisor to the debate club."

"It doesn't exist," I told her. "I'm advising it on paper, but there's no club anymore. I'm out of the game now."

Rozlyn was collecting her book, returning it to her backpack.

"Do you ever miss it?" she asked.

"All the time."

"Huh," she mused. She was standing up, slinging the laden backpack over her shoulder. "But no debate club at BYU?"

"'Fraid not," I told her.

"Well," she said, sliding out the door, "I guess I'll have to look for some other source of meaning in my life." The door swung shut behind her.

"I've been looking for twenty years," I yelled through the office wall, turning back around to face my desk.

A second later, there was another soft tap at my door. As I turned around, Rozlyn pulled the door open enough to look back inside.

"Twenty years?" she asked.

"Give or take."

And she sat down again and told me the stories of some tournaments she had won.

3

No one loves being in class. No matter how committed you are to participating in class, there is just too much of it. If you doubt it, consider this: Teachers require class. No one requires students to go to football games or parties. The existence of rules tells you something about what people really want to do.

If you're a student, you can manage the excess of class days by skipping a few. (No requirement to attend class is so draconian that it doesn't allow for a little leeway.) But if you're teaching, there's no getting around it. If other people have to sit through your class, then you have to show up too.

The darkest time of the semester, at least in Utah, is in the middle of winter term. Students have been going to school for months, but the glimmer of summer is still too far away to reflect any hope in the present.

On one of these days, I was talking about the early Ralph Waldo Emerson to a lecture hall of listless students. In his early essays, Emerson was most exercised in his antagonism to thoughtless conformity. When your choices are determined by something other than the exercise of your own capacities, they don't reveal anything about you. Emerson thought you could interact with someone a lot and yet remain a stranger to them, all because your interactions didn't really say anything about you *in particular*.

Emerson's essays—often originating as lectures—are meant to be heard more than read. It would hardly make sense to browbeat someone into accepting the belief that they should make up their own mind. Emerson appreciated this problem and so framed his arguments as deliberate provocation. He was less interested in persuading people and more interested in shaking them up enough to do some thinking on their own. Here's what I have in mind: "The orator distrusts at first the fitness of his frank confessions,—his want of knowledge of the persons he addresses, —until he finds that he is the complement of his hearers;—that they drink from his words because he fulfils for them their own nature; the deeper he dives into his privatest, secretest presentiment, to his wonder he finds, this is the most acceptable, most public, and universally true. The people delight in it; the better part of every man feels, This is my music; this is myself."[4]

It's a little hard to make out what is happening in this passage, precisely because it is written in the cadence of an urgent speech. The clauses all strung together, pushing forward without any time for a sentence break, show the speaker really cares about getting something across.

Emerson is here at pains to point out that, contrary to what we might expect, people identify more with the private workings of another's mind than they do with the person's public self-presentation. The parts of ourselves we think of as idiosyncratic and strange are more, not less, recognizable to others.

As I was explaining all this, I meandered to the back of the classroom.

"It's all too easy to drift into conventions without thinking about it at all," I said, looking around the room. "Who's sitting in exactly the same seat they happened to sit down in on the first day?"

"Could you remember who we were if we weren't?" a student queried.

---

4. Ralph Waldo Emerson, *Ralph Waldo Emerson: Essays and Lectures*, Library of America 15 (New York: Literary Classics of the United States, 1983), 64–65.

"Stop undermining my point, Madilyn!"

"Madison," she corrected.

"Here's another example," I pushed on. Emerson says that we're always worried about doing the reading, but really doing the reading is just as likely to be harmful as beneficial. The problem with doing the reading is that we're always trying to figure out what the author thought rather than what we thought."

A student raised his hand from near the back of the room. "Xander!" I said.

"So, Emerson was against reading?" he asked, hopefully. It sounded like this was the kind of philosophy he might be able to get behind.

"Well, he was against reading if it stopped you from thinking about what you believed. Remember, he said every sentence was supposed to be 'doubly significant.' The first significance is what you thought it meant to the author, and the second significance is what it meant to you."[5]

"What's the difference?" Xander pressed.

"Let me give you an example from my own life," I said. "Who here has seen *Butch Cassidy and the Sundance Kid*?" A smattering of hands went up. "When I was growing up," I continued, "it was my parents' favorite movie. There's a scene in it where Butch and Sundance are trying to get jobs as payroll guards. There's this old-timer who's interviewing them, trying to decide if they're up to it. He notices Sundance is wearing a handgun, and the old-timer asks if he can hit anything. Sundance modestly says that sometimes he can. The old-timer takes the gun out of his holster and hands it to him, directing him to shoot the can down the street. Sundance shoots a few rounds, missing every time. The old man shakes his head, and he starts walking away. But then Sundance calls back, 'Can I move?' And the old

5. Emerson, *Essays and Lectures*, 57.

man is like, 'What do you mean?' With that, Sundance draws his holstered gun and shoots the can, and then shoots it again and again while it's still in the air. The old-timer is stunned. And then Sundance says, 'I'm better when I move.'

"Anyway, when I was growing up, my parents would quote that line all the time. And to them, it wasn't just about shooting. They'd say it whenever you needed to stop overthinking something. Sometimes if we stop thinking self-consciously about some activity, we'll do it more effectively than if we focus on each part of what we're doing. If you plan too much, or if you think too hard, it can make you worse. You're better when you move."

After class, Xander came up to me. "*Butch Cassidy* is my family's favorite movie too."

"Where are you from?" I asked him.

"Idaho."

I nodded.

"We actually quote that same line, in my family," he told me.

"It's a good line," I said.

◆ ◆ ◆

A few weeks later, as I was walking into class, a student from the front row rushed up to me.

"Dr. Davis!" he said, "Something is happening!"

"What's that?" I asked.

"Some students have taken over the front row!"

"Taken over?"

"Yes!"

"What does it mean to *take over* a row?"

"They're sitting in every chair on the front row and won't leave."

By this point in the conversation, we had arrived at the front row. And in fact, there were students in every seat.

"What's happening?" I asked.

"We changed up where we sit," Aerin answered with a shrug, a bit mischievously.

I later learned that she and a couple of her friends from class had recruited enough people—including a few students I had never seen before—to fill every single chair of the front row of the lecture hall. When the previous class had ended, they filed in immediately and waited for departing students to leave.

As I arrived at the scene, a couple of front row usuals joined the protest. Trying to suppress my appreciation of the gimmick in the face of their apparent seriousness, I confessed that I was powerless to stop the claim jumpers. There were no assigned seats in the class. Everything was first come, first served. Still, I was curious about what was happening.

"What came over you to do this?" I asked.

Aerin shrugged again. "Just got tired of conformity, I guess."

4

The clock on the classroom wall said 11:01.

"OK, we're starting," I said, to little avail. "This is me, starting!" The murmur of conversation around the classroom on a Monday morning subsided a little.

"Here are some questions to review! Question 1: Does anybody remember the difference between perfect procedural justice and pure procedural justice?"

A single hand went up near the front of the classroom.

"Rozlyn!" I said.

"Perfect procedural justice is when there's an independent fact about what's just and a procedure to find it, and pure procedural justice is when there's only a procedure."

"Good," I said. "Next question: Will parties behind the veil of ignorance ever think that utilitarianism is just?"

"No!" It was the same voice from the center of class.

"Why not?" I asked.

Rozlyn raised her hand. I took a long look around the classroom, looking for someone else to call on. Eventually my glance circled back, and she gestured with a half smile to her still-raised arm.

"Rozlyn," I said.

"Utilitarianism will let good things for some people outweigh bad things for other people, no matter how bad those things are. And with the veil of ignorance, no one would risk ending up as one of the unlucky ones," she explained.

"OK," I said, "this next one is specifically for not-Rozlyn members of this class."

5

The clock on the conference room wall read 5:12. The week's meeting was drawing to a close. We had just finished distributing all of the papers to be graded.

"Are you sure you can manage all of that grading?" I asked Quinn. He was also applying for medical schools that semester, and he already had some visits planned.

"Oh yeah," he said. "It gives me a break from doing other stuff, so it's not too bad."

"Well, thank you!" I said. "Sometimes a change is as good as a rest."

"Ha!" he said. "My dad says that."

"My dad says it!" I countered.

"Really?"

"Where is your dad from?" I asked.

"Blackfoot, Idaho."

"Ha!" I declared. "My dad is from Blackfoot, Idaho."

He nodded as if this made sense.

"Wait," I said. I pointed back and forth between us. "Are we brothers?"

"I think it's probably just something people say in Blackfoot," he said.

"Maybe Blackfoot is just a place where people need a change," I offered.

"Or a rest," he observed.

6

The classroom clock said 11:02. "OK!" I said, "who wants some review questions?" There was a dull, indecipherable sound that amounted, I suppose, to a reply. For the most part, students avoided eye contact. Waiting for a moment, I glanced around the room to see who was showing up on Friday morning.

"Rozlyn?" I asked. She nodded as if to acknowledge my question.

"Weren't you just here for the last hour of this very class?" She leaned forward slightly. "I need this today," she said.

"OK!" I started again. "What's the ambiguous premise in Nozick's Wilt Chamberlain argument?"

One hand went up.

7

When the semester ended, I saw both Aerin (of the second-row coup) and Xander again. Aerin and her friends stopped by to give me a new laser pointer for lectures, having observed my frustration with the unreliability of the one in the classroom. Xander stopped by my office to present me with a wooden box. The lid was engraved:

Doctor Ryan Davis
"BETTER WHEN I MOVE"

I opened the box, and inside was a pocketknife. On one side was engraved an image of a dry fly one might use in fly-fishing. On the other side, a pheasant in flight.

I never saw Xander again, but a few years later he did reappear in my life. He had found—he believed—the one girl in Idaho who shared all of my values, and also my particular sensibility. Being well-versed in the practices of shared religion, he felt responsible to alert us to this fact. And he wasn't wrong, although his words had a significance different from the one he might have intended. He had met my favorite cousin.

8

I slipped into the back of the auditorium and took a seat in the back row. Jamie was running the review session before the final exam. Only this time, rather than doing the review as a series of PowerPoint slides reviewing each author, Jamie had created an entire Kahoot! game of trivia questions based on authors from modern political philosophy. As the game proceeded, I began to notice that the top three contestants were getting the question right round after round. I noticed also that the people around me were noticing as well, until eventually a cheer went up whenever we'd see that the top scorers had gotten the question right yet again. There could only be one winner, though, and eventually two of the three top contestants made errors. Jamie declared the victor, and—to the surprise of everyone in the room—asked the winner to come down to the front of the class. There, she presented the champion with a certificate bearing all of the TAs' signatures, as well as my own.

The next day I walked into the TA meeting and saw Jamie there.

"That girl who won Kahoot! seemed so happy!" I said.

"Oh, you don't even know!" Jamie replied. She pulled out her phone. A moment later, the rest of our phones buzzed with a message. I opened it to find a picture of Jamie's certificate posted on the student's Instagram account. There, in formal letters on the certificate's distinguished manilla parchment, were the following words:

POLI 202 KAHOOT! CHAMPION!

Below the caption were all of our signatures, attesting to the document's authenticity. The caption below the picture read, "Easily the third proudest moment of my life."

"Awww," Adrienne said. "It really mattered to her."

"That's right," I agreed. "You can tell because she gives the ranking. If she had just said, 'proudest moment of my whole life,' it would sound like hyperbole. But the fact that she can think of only two better ones"—I nodded at Jamie—"shows she really cared about winning this." I paused for a moment, admiring the Instagram post. "All the work we do for the class, and the thing that mattered the most for this student was something we'd never even thought to do before."

"Well, it is a pretty nice certificate," Jamie agreed.

"What inspired you to make it?" I asked.

She shrugged. "It's actually really easy to make certificates at University Printing," she said.

"The third proudest moment of her life . . ." I mused. "And it wasn't even part of your job to do it."

"Well, that's not always what matters."

"That's the thing they don't tell you," I said. "The thing they don't tell you is that nothing you're paid to do is what matters, and nothing that matters is something you're paid to do."

Jamie nodded from side to side, as if to give the claim a fair hearing.

"What's the argument for that?"

9

The clock in the conference room read 4:06.

"The third game, I was playing black and was down a pawn in the endgame but still managed a draw," Luke was explaining.

"Nice work," Brad nodded.

"I've been thinking about trying a new opening against 1.d4."

"What's that?"

The door in the back opened, and Adrienne walked in and found a chair, swinging her backpack from her shoulder. It landed on the table with a thud. She put her hands down on the table, leaning slightly forward.

"Guys!" she said. Everyone looked at her. "I watched *La La Land*." She paused for just a moment, ensuring that she had the room's attention. "Jessica Flanigan was right. Dr. Davis doesn't understand his own favorite movie!"

CHAPTER 8

Divine Riddles in the Laser-Tag Line

So shall my word be that goes out from my mouth;
it shall not return to me empty,
but it shall accomplish that which I purpose,
and succeed in the thing for which I sent it.

—Isaiah 55:11

"Finally, I was tired enough to have lost all sense of inhibition."
It's 9:00 a.m., Sunday, March 21, 2021. Although I too am tired,
the previous sentence is not about me. I'm in church, listening
to the opening talk of the morning. (And unlike the first speaker
in today's meeting, my Sunday morning fatigue is not associated
with a lack of inhibition.) Most talks begin with a meandering
apology for the ten minutes of boredom the speaker is about to
inflict upon the audience. "I don't like this any more than you
do" is the orthopraxical sentiment with which to start a talk in
a Latter-day Saint worship service.[1]

---

1. This is the opposite of musical performances. In a musical performance in church, the performer is expected to try very hard and sincerely,
and the listeners expect to enjoy it. In a talk, it's vaguely counternormative
to try—as if trying involved the implicit assertion that the speaker knew
more than the listeners about the topic at hand. That would be impolite.

However, this beginning is unusual. The talk at the center of this essay opens with pace and direction. The speaker has something to say.

It's important to get the story right, and I've already broken it up too much, so let's start again. "Finally, I was tired enough to have lost all sense of inhibition." The speaker starts not at the story's beginning but in its middle. There's no word of introduction about what we should expect to find ahead. But the speaker does give us some details. The story is set several years ago, and the occasion is the night of high school graduation.[2]

The official ceremonies are long over, and our speaker is at a party. By the time of the story's opening line, it's one o'clock the next morning. I don't know exactly how I know this, but I have the sense during the talk that the party is great, that the speaker has many friends, that her school life had been prosperous.

At one in the morning, though, something changes. Our protagonist hears the voice of God. Well, not God's voice, precisely. Within our religious tradition, it's not common for the recipient of a spiritual directive to hear a voice in the standard, audible sense in which we hear the verbal utterances of those around us under ordinary conditions. There's not meant to be any dishonor in this. In fact, it might be that nonauditory speaking is in some way deeper or more urgent. In the Book of Mormon's most central moment, when Jesus himself appears to the Nephites, his arrival is announced by God. Here's how the voice of God is described: "[I]t was not a harsh voice, neither was it a loud voice; nevertheless, and notwithstanding it being a small voice it did pierce them that did hear to the center, insomuch that there was no part of their frame that it did not cause to

---

2. Most of my fellow congregants are college students. At BYU, it remains common for students to be married by the midway point in their college career, so it's also normal for new couples in my ward to be college age.

quake; yea, it did pierce them to the very soul, and did cause their hearts to burn" (3 Nephi 11:3).

The first part of this passage makes it sound like hearing the voice of God is an auditory experience—the voice is quiet, but still a voice in the ordinary sense. But then things get a little more enigmatic. The voice of God is felt more than it is heard. It affects the hearer in a physical way, notwithstanding the listeners hadn't yet even been able to make out the words that the voice was saying (cf. 3 Nephi 11:4). The voice of God is heard in the heart more than in the ear.

A way of putting this kind of experience is to say that one hears the voice of the Spirit. And this is what the speaker reports. She is at the party, and she is impressed by the Spirit: "Go check on Alicia." Even if not auditory, the voice in question is linguistic. The speaker shifts her cadence in the retelling as if to suggest that the quotation is taken verbatim.

It's a commonplace in stories like this for the hearer to wait for further promptings before acting. The voice of God is so startling in its mystery that even the devout can be left momentarily uncertain. Think of the young Samuel being repeatedly awakened from a deep sleep with his divine commission. With no prior prophetic experience, he must ask the priest Eli what is happening (1 Samuel 3). As in the Samuel story, the Nephites must hear the voice speak three times before they discern what it is saying. But in the story of this particular Sunday morning, our protagonist simply does as the Spirit prompts. She leaves the party and goes in search of her friend.

It turns out Alicia is fine. Our speaker finds her in line for laser tag, which apparently as recently as a few years ago was still open for business in the small hours of the morning, at least on the night of graduation. In any case, nothing at all is wrong with Alicia. She isn't alone or sad or worried or about to be in any kind of trouble. There's no indication that she's in need of a friend at all. In fact, after the speaker joins the queue for laser tag, Alicia takes advantage of the situation and leaves her friend holding their place in line. Our protagonist watches as Alicia wanders off and starts to talk with some boys. She's had enough. She goes to confront Alicia. "What are you doing?" she asks her friend, perhaps a bit sharply. "We've had enough of this for one night!" I can't tell you whether we're meant to hear this reproof with a bit of a friendly wink—whether it's just a bit of casual ribbing or actually sincere upbraiding.

We are given no indication about how Alicia responds. This is because our protagonist is already turning around, on her way back to her place in line. But as she about-faces to walk away, she comes face to face with another person. "I'm Matt," he says. I don't know what expression our speaker had on her face as she notices for the first time the very real person who had arrived behind her. Apparently, Matt had overheard enough of the speaker's exchange that he felt some pressure to introduce himself in turn. I also have no idea what our protagonist says back. The next line of the story is not directed to Matt but to us, her listeners. "That night I learned his last name," she confides, "and by the end of that month I wanted to take it."

Even now, some four years on, our protagonist says that line so unflinchingly that I hear my own breath come up short. And I'm just somebody sitting in the pews on Sunday morning listening to the sermonized version of the story.

The Puzzle

I've seen enough episodes of *Gilmore Girls* to know how the story goes from there. Our protagonist has just met the love of her life. And Matt is, in fact, the young husband sitting supportively behind her now, this Sunday morning half a decade later. The issue is not how the story winds its way from the laser-tag place to this chapel on the south side of Provo. Cutting off the narrative where she does gives a sense of inevitability to whatever events ensued. The question is about how to interpret the Spirit's voice. No offense to Alicia, but we all now know that this wasn't her story. Yet the Spirit sent our protagonist to check on her. Why would God do that?

This is, of course, a very old sort of question. More than a few to whom God has spoken have wondered why that strange voice puzzles as often as it illuminates—maybe more often. Well before this Sunday morning, people have tried to make sense of why God speaks in riddles.

I will get back to the speaker's own answer in a minute. To set it up, it will help us to consider some earlier efforts. One of the most famous is in Mark 4. There, Jesus has just finished giving the parable of the sower. You recall the parable. A sower goes out to sow seeds, and some fall on the path and are quickly eaten by birds. Other seeds fall on rocky ground, where they quickly grow but then die in the heat of the sun. Other seeds fall among thorns, which choke the seedlings as they begin to grow. None of these yield any grain. But some seeds fall on good ground, and these produce a harvest of "thirty and sixty and a hundredfold" (4:8). Commentators on this passage note that any of these yields far surpasses what Jesus's listeners would have anticipated, which would probably have been around a seven-to-one ratio. So, even with all the seeds that perish, the sower's work succeeds beyond any expectation.

Jesus tells this parable to the "very large crowd" (4:1) gathered by the seashore, which provides the initial setting for the chapter. Parables are among the teachings mostly commonly attributed to the historical Jesus. The term is from the Greek *parabole*, which just means "throwing alongside."³ Parables provide a kind of extended metaphor in which a teaching about the arrival of God's kingdom is thrown alongside of—or concealed within—a story about mundane life. When they're once again alone, his disciples ask him why he chooses this method. Why not just say the message he meant to say outright? Jesus's response is interesting. He replies:

> "To you has been given the secret of the kingdom of God, but for those outside, everything comes in parables; in order that
> 'they may indeed look, but not perceive
> and may indeed listen, but not understand;
> so that they may not turn again and be forgiven.'"
> (Mark 4:10-12)

What's going on? Jesus sounds like he's saying that he wants outsiders to *not* get what he's saying, lest they repent and receive God's forgiveness. But that makes it seem as if he is trying to *prevent* the crowd from converting to his own message, which would be an unusual tack for any teacher to take. The last half of Jesus's answer is a quotation from Isaiah 6:9-10. That is the chapter in which Isaiah receives his commission, which includes an apparent instruction to stop the people from accepting God's word:

> "Make the mind of this people dull,
> and stop their ears,
> and shut their eyes,
> so that they may not look with their eyes,

3. Amy-Jill Levine and Marc Zvi Brettler, eds., *The Jewish Annotated New Testament*, 2nd ed. (Oxford: Oxford University Press, 2017), 68.

> and listen with their ears,
> and comprehend with their minds,
> and turn and be healed."   (Isaiah 6:10)

This—and the negotiation between Isaiah and God that follows—is certainly a strange and mysterious passage in a strange and mysterious book. On its surface, it looks like God is telling the prophet to thwart all of the different ways in which his listeners might perceive God's voice, whatever form that voice might take. Don't let them hear it *or* see it *or* even apprehend it nonverbally! Whatever we make of that, the question now before us is whether Jesus means something along the same lines. That appears to be how Mark made sense of Jesus's teachings. Mark was writing after the destruction of the temple in Jerusalem—decades after the death of Jesus. From his point of view, it was obvious that the message of Jesus would be widely rejected. From start to finish, Mark is a long procession of increasingly important agents rejecting Jesus. (A fact which makes the evangelist's concluding call to faith all the more dramatic.) We see this already in Mark 7, where "the Pharisees and some of the scribes" (7:1) openly confront Jesus and his followers.

Back to our question: Why does Jesus speak in parables? We can now give one possible answer. He speaks in parables as a way of counterrejecting his enemies, who already oppose him. John Dominic Crossan writes that "for Mark, parables intend to reject those who have already rejected Jesus."[4]

For his part, Crossan thinks Mark is getting Jesus wrong. Jesus, even as presented within Mark's own Gospel, appears to *want* his listeners to hear and accept his message. Mere verses later, he gives the parable of the lampstand, which is about

4. John Dominic Crossan, *The Power of Parable: How Fiction by Jesus Became Fiction about Jesus* (San Francisco: HarperOne, 2013), 23.

exactly the opposite: revealing God's kingdom rather than hiding it. And it's not for nothing that Jesus begins his parable with an imperative—"Listen!" (4:3)—even when he is talking to the crowd as a whole. And the very last verse of this section (4:34) suggests that Jesus continues speaking to "them"—the crowd—in parables "as they were able to hear it" (4:33). Crossan interprets this to mean that some in the crowd *did* understand the parables. And finally, there's the parable of the sower itself. Wasn't the parable about a sower trying to sow seeds, not a sower trying to stop seeds from being sown? By having Jesus say that he is trying to conceal his message, Mark seems to be reading the parable itself against the grain. Mark's way of making sense of Jesus's words, then, is better understood as a kind of historical retrospective—a way of coming to terms with Jesus after he had been rejected, not as a way of interpreting his intentions when speaking at the time. Crossan concludes, "This is not a program for incomprehension."[5]

So far, we've looked at the parable of the sower for help in understanding the question of why God sometimes speaks in a confusing way. But now it seems like we've only made matters worse. If Crossan is right, Mark thinks that God speaks with the aim to conceal, but that has more to do with Mark's own human perspective than with the aims and plans of his story's central character. So, on Crossan's rereading of Mark's reading of Jesus, God isn't the one doing the concealing.

Of course, that reading of the parable is fraught with controversy. Not everyone accepts Crossan's way of separating Jesus's aims in telling the parable from Mark's aims in recounting Jesus's aims. N. T. Wright thinks the parable of the sower is meant to tell us something about God's plan for Israel. For Wright, the crucial background text is Isaiah 55. Isaiah there

---

5. Crossan, *Power of Parable*, 25.

compares the rain and snow to the word of God. Rain and snow give "seed to the sower and bread to the eater" (55:10). The word of God brings something even more important than physical nourishment. When people hear the word, they can know that God is still with Israel; God has not cut off his people.

And here is where it gets more interesting. The parable is not just describing the word of God. *The parable is, itself, among God's words.* More than that, the parable employs God's word in the task of separating out those who "have ears to hear" from those who misunderstand and reject it, and in so doing it participates in the very process it describes: the much-anticipated prelude to the return of God's kingdom. As Wright puts it, "the parable, therefore, not only informs, but, as has been pointed out often enough, it *acts*."[6]

Seen this way, the parable really is threatening. By helping inaugurate the Kingdom of Heaven, it issues a challenge (locally) to Herod, and (generally) to imperial Rome. Indeed, it challenges the authority of all earthly power as organized in political states. Wright explains: "'If you have ears, then hear'; if too many understood too well, the prophet's liberty of movement, and perhaps life, may be cut short. Jesus knew his kingdom-announcement was subversive. It would be drastically unwelcome, for different reasons, to the Romans, to Herod, and also to zealous Jews and their leaders, whether official or not. He must therefore speak in parables. Only those in the know must be allowed to glimpse what Jesus believed was going on."[7]

For Wright, then, Mark believes that Jesus is trying to conceal his message from some, and Mark is correct about that. Jesus needs to conceal his message because what he has to say

---

6. N. T. Wright, *Jesus and the Victory of God*, vol. 2 of *Christian Origins and the Question of God* (Minneapolis: Fortress, 1997), 234.

7. Wright, *Jesus and the Victory of God*, 237.

is politically explosive. God must both communicate the truth to some and conceal it from others. To put it metaphorically, the parable kills two birds with one stone.[8]

The Answer

Back to our story. God's revelation often puzzles, but none of the explanations so far makes sense of the night after graduation. We can easily imagine her story involving crowds, doubting outsiders, and suspicious authority figures. But even if those figures were all there, none of them hear the Spirit's words at all. As far as we know, our protagonist was the only person to receive the divine directive, so there was no reason for the Spirit to camouflage it against potential meddlers.

So, what was God up to? In her reflection on the story, the speaker explains that the most important thing in the story is that she and her future husband encounter each other in their "true selves." It was crucial that, somehow or other, he would see who she really was. This is, after all, a love story of sorts. And love for another person is a lot about seeing them for who they are. The speaker's point here might well have been echoing Iris Murdoch, who famously described loving someone as a way of really seeing them.[9]

When you meet the love of your life, that person is supposed to fall for you *as you*—not for the way you present yourself in public. The latter is a persona deployed to get along, keep out of the way, or otherwise conceal who you really are. This isn't just the stuff of romantic comedies. The ideal of love is about attending to a person's real traits, even when those might not

8. Or, if you prefer, feeds two birds with one scone.
9. I talk about this more in chapter 4.

be the ones we usually idealize. In a comment about Murdoch's conception of love, the philosopher Vida Yao elaborates: "According to Murdoch, the task of really *seeing* another person accurately and justly is a moral achievement as it takes seeing past our 'fat, relentless' egos in order to recognize another person as part of a reality that exists beyond ourselves. It is to resist seeing him tainted and shaped by our fears, needs, and (typically narcissistic) fantasies."[10]

Yao then adds an important qualification: "I agree with Murdoch. But it is important not to forget that attentive love is not just an ideal because it involves a moral and epistemological improvement in the lover, but because it provides the beloved with the sense that he—who he really or most fully or deeply is—is the object of another's loving attention. He can let down his guard, and let the other in."[11]

Murdoch's point is that loving someone involves seeing their real self. What Yao is pointing out here is that this isn't just a matter of importance for the one who loves—of getting it right or seeing the truth, as it were. It's also important for the one who is loved, because this kind of love—what Yao is calling attentive love—offers the kind of security that makes a loving relationship possible.

Anyhow, what does seeing another's true self have to do with the Spirit's (mis)directing our protagonist to check on Alicia? Recall the talk's opening line: "Finally, I was tired enough to have lost all sense of inhibition." At long last, after all the day's activities, she had reached the point where her inhibitions were gone—worn down by some combination of achievement, happiness, and exhaustion. Her future spouse

10. Vida Yao, "Grace and Alienation," *Philosopher's Imprint* 20, no. 16 (2020): 6–7, https://tinyurl.com/ymxtamz4. Italics original.
11. Yao, "Grace and Alienation," 7.

encounters her when he overhears her dressing down Alicia in the laser-tag line. It's a fleeting moment when her true self is visible. Our protagonist was brought exactly next to an important person in the story of her life but without confronting him directly. It's as if the Spirit knew just how to throw our protagonist alongside her future love.

Now imagine if, instead, the Spirit had been straight about it. Imagine if there had been no puzzle. God might have said: "The time has come! I'm about to introduce you to the love of your life. Get thee to the laser-tag place!" Certainly, there have been stranger divine directives. But as she tells the story, our protagonist suggests that things might not have gone well. Who, after all, can be their real self when all the pressure of the whole future of their life is suddenly, unexpectedly upon them in one moment? That's an impossible ask.

Of course, the Spirit would have known that. So, suppose the directive had been modified slightly, to take this into account: "Go now to the laser-tag place, and there you will meet the love of your life. But for heaven's sake be cool about it!" This is no better and almost certainly worse. I don't know about you, but my own experience of being a person is that nothing is more impossible than playing it cool on command. No spirit would inspire someone in that sort of way.

So, what is the interpretation of the story? The speaker makes sense of it this way. God tells her to go check on Alicia, and she forms the false belief that something is the matter with Alicia. That way, when the critical moment arrives, she and Matt can see each other for who they really are. She acts in the way that she ought to act, which is to be her authentic self. But in this peculiar case, she can act that way only if she misunderstands the situation. The Spirit leads her into having exactly the wrong belief that will facilitate right action. She notes later in the talk that she and Matt had traveled in similar circles in high school, but she suspects that if they had met earlier, it wouldn't have worked out. God prevented them from meeting until the moment when God guided them to meet.

The point of the riddle of the laser-tag line has something in common with both Crossan's and Wright's readings of the parable of the sower but fits neither one exactly. As in Crossan's interpretation of Mark, the Spirit in this story wants our protagonist to form a slightly misguided belief about what's going on. But, unlike with Mark's Jesus, God does this not out of rejection but out of love. Sometimes, you keep people from the truth not to foil their ends but to honor them. Like Wright's Jesus, what the Spirit really cares about is action. It's a mistake to see the Spirit as a kind of cosmic repository of facts. We should interpret God as an active participant with whom cooperation is not only possible but a core objective of religious life. Unlike in Wright's reading of the parable, here the reason for concealing the message has nothing to do with withholding it from any malevolent third parties. The modern world—or at least the small corner of it wherein this story is set—is less about external threats and more about how parts of ourselves can jeopardize our own authentic self-revelation. God speaks in riddles not to separate the believers from the wicked but rather to separate the believing parts of us (who we're growing into) from the troublesome parts (who we're growing away from).[12] Or at least that's how I understand the interpretation as given on this particular Sunday morning.

12. Here I'm drawing on Jessica Flanigan's interpretation of parables. See also Agnes Callard, *Aspiration: The Agency of Becoming* (New York: Oxford University Press, 2018).

A Problem

"Does this mean the Spirit was manipulating me?" our speaker asks. The thing I most admire about her talk is that it confronts this question head on. It's a fair question. The Spirit *does* seem to lead our protagonist into misunderstanding her situation. And when you get someone to do what you want them to do by leading them into having a mistaken understanding of the situation they're in—that's just what we call manipulation.[13]

But wait a second. All the Spirit said was that our protagonist should go check on Alicia. And in fact, it was true that going to check on Alicia was a really good idea. So, what's the issue? The speaker formed a true belief (that she ought to go check on Alicia) that was also justified by her evidence (prompting by the Spirit). All the way back to Plato, people have understood knowledge in terms of justified, true beliefs. If you believe something that's both true and justified, then you know it. On that standard, it seems like the Spirit helps our protagonist know the truth, and indeed she does come to know it. And so, we might think, God didn't do anything manipulative.

You might think this sounds like a suspiciously easy way out. The Spirit does not precisely speak any falsehoods, but that seems to be slightly missing the point. We can sharpen this problem with just a little conceptual refinement. In one of the most famous philosophy papers of the twentieth century, Edmund Gettier challenged the ancient idea that knowledge could be analyzed as justified, true belief. Gettier offered a few counterexamples, in which a person has a justified, true belief about something, and yet this belief does not intuitively seem to count as knowledge.

13. Onora O'Neill, "Between Consenting Adults," *Philosophy & Public Affairs* 14, no. 3 (1985): 252–77; Christian Coons and Michael Weber, eds., *Manipulation: Theory and Practice* (Oxford: Oxford University Press, 2014).

Suppose—to use a famous example—you find yourself wondering what time it is in the afternoon. (Maybe you're in a meeting.) You look up and see a clock on the wall that reads 3:37. You form the belief that it is 3:37 p.m., and in fact you're right; it is 3:37. Success! However, unbeknownst to you, the clock on the wall is broken, and it was just by chance that you looked at it during one of two minutes that day when it told the correct time.

Did you really know it was 3:37 p.m. after checking the clock? Many people—even across different cultures—will answer that you did not. You had the right belief, but you just lucked into the right belief. You didn't know it to be true.[14]

Now, let's return to the laser-tag line. Does our protagonist know that she should go check on Alicia? She believes she ought to go check on Alicia, and her belief is true and justified. However, it seems like in the standard Gettier cases, she doesn't really know it, because she has been led to form her belief in

---

14. If you're wondering how psychologists test this sort of thing, here's a longer example:

> Paul Jones was worried because it was 10 pm and his wife Mary was not home from work yet. Usually she is home by 6 pm. He tried her cell phone but just kept getting her voicemail. Starting to worry that something might have happened to her, he decided to call some local hospitals to ask whether any patient by the name of "Mary Jones" had been admitted that evening. At the University Hospital, the person who answered his call confirmed that someone by that name had been admitted with major but not life-threatening injuries following a car crash. Paul grabbed his coat and rushed out to drive to University hospital [*sic*]. As it turned out, the patient at University Hospital was not Paul's wife, but another woman with the same name. In fact, Paul's wife had a heart attack as she was leaving work, and was at that moment receiving treatment in Metropolitan Hospital, a few miles away.

> Does Paul know that his wife is in the hospital? Even though he truly believes she is in the hospital, most people will respond to this prompt by saying that he doesn't know it. See Edouard Machery et al., "Gettier Across Cultures," *Noûs* 51, no. 3 (2017): 648, https://tinyurl.com/2ta5wp7f.

a confusing way. She gets to a true belief (that she should go check on Alicia) by way of adopting a false belief (that Alicia needs help). And if God were misleading her in a way to get her to do the right thing, then it still seems—on our earlier account of manipulation—like she is being manipulated.

Working It Out

Don't worry. We're close to the end now. I just want to relay the talk's final thought, which is to propose a solution to this problem. Our speaker says that it *would* be manipulative if God were trying to bring about our obedience to guidance that doesn't let us in on what's really going on. But we know that God is perfect, and a perfect God would not manipulate us. So, we can infer that God must not be trying to secure our obedience. The speaker says that revelation is not the "independent variable" that brings about our obedience. I take this to mean that God does not intend the revelation to be issued as a command. If it were so issued, it would be manipulative. But God does want us to do what's good for us. God's authority, then, must be merely epistemic.[15] God is like the person who gives a very good tip that we happen to overhear. That person is not issuing you an order. They're just tossing seeds out and seeing what comes up. God is basically saying, (1) I love you, and (2) I'm just putting this out there.

So, the talk is not revisionist about whether we should do what God says. We should do what God says. Who wants to miss the chance encounter with the love of their life at the precisely perfect moment?

15. See Stephen Darwall, *The Second-Person Standpoint: Morality, Respect, and Accountability* (Cambridge, MA: Harvard University Press, 2006).

Chapter 8

End

Let's take stock. What did we learn? We started out trying to make sense of a puzzle about revelation. Why does revelation take the form of riddles? The answer to that was that we need the riddles to get ourselves to act in the practically rational way. Without the riddles, we'd just have true beliefs. It seems like true beliefs are just what we need, but that's a mistake. Sometimes—in fact in very important times—true beliefs can lead us into practical disaster. So, the Spirit of God sometimes gives us riddles that lead the acting part of us to do what is best while the believing part of us is left scratching our head about it—at least till we get a better vantage point after the fact.

This turned up an insight about the authority of God. God's authority is not that of a practical command. God knows what we need to do. That's why God's revelation leaves us free to act. We might have thought that we were free to act in the sense that God wouldn't make us do the right thing. But it's actually stronger than that: God doesn't even make the thing that we should do the right thing. In other words, at least a lot of what God says is not by way of command at all. God doesn't physically force us, *and* God doesn't force us morally. He just gives us the information that we need—just enough and not any too much—in order to act in the way that will make our lives go in the way we want. The final lesson from our speaker's text might be this: that's what God wants too.

CHAPTER 9

Family Home Evening,
or How I Learned to Stop Worrying
and Love Quietist Theological Relativism

Sometimes I'm convinced by a single sentence to believe the opposite of what I had believed up till the moment before. I met Charles after church one week during the first summer I spent in Utah. He asked about my plan to start teaching at BYU. He was a professor at Tufts, though on his visits to Utah he was especially interested in finding places to fish.

"People think that fishing takes patience," he said.

"What does it actually take?" I asked him.

"Just the opposite," he replied. "Fishing takes *impatience*."

"Why do you say that?" I followed up. He considered the question.

"You have to keep trying different things. If you're patient, you'll never figure out what works."

"Huh," I said. "I suppose that's right."

I've been explaining fishing to outsiders in this way ever since.

The End of the World, Plan B

Charles visited Utah from Massachusetts. While in town, he offered the lesson for an extended family home evening. His title was "The End of the World, Plan B," which was also the name of a course he taught on comparative religion, as well as a book he had recently finished.[1]

The first thing is to understand plan A. According to Charles, plan A for the end of the world was for justice to be served—for the wicked to be punished and the righteous to be rewarded. Many religious traditions anticipate a world-ending apocalypse—or an event John Dominic Crossan likes to call the "great clean up" at the end of the world.[2] But there is a problem with this plan. The issue is not that justice won't be served—that things won't actually get cleaned up in the last act. Rather, the problem is that the meting out of justice won't be as satisfying for us then as we imagine it will be now. Here, I'm summarizing Charles's point, so I may not be getting things exactly right. This is just the recollection of one person.

To doubt whether justice will provide us with everything we hoped for is not to say we should be indifferent to justice. Certainly, we should do what we can to make the world just. What we can't count on is for justice to fill a gap in the meaning of our lives.

Why not? The answer is that demanding justice is bad for us in something akin to the way that injustice was bad for us in the first place. Injustice is bad in part because it makes us feel servile to or dependent on someone else. When others wrong us, they treat us in a way that they are not entitled to. We have the right to demand that they respect our claims to justice. When they don't, it can make us feel like we depend on their discretion for our moral rights to be protected. And that's a bad feeling.

1. Charles Shiro Inouye, *The End of the World, Plan B: A Guide for the Future* (Salt Lake City, UT: Greg Kofford Books, 2016).
2. John Dominic Crossan, *God and Empire: Jesus against Rome, Then and Now* (San Francisco: HarperOne, 2007).

Next, consider the sensation of seeing justice done. Everyone likes to see the villain get his comeuppance at the end of the movie. But there's a bit of a catch to this feeling. We not only want to see the villain get what he deserves; we also want the villain to *know* he's getting what he deserves. In a telling example, the philosopher Dan Moller asks us to imagine a movie where the hero's nemesis finally reaps what he has sown. Only, this time the villain doesn't have any comprehension of his misfortune as a consequence of prior misdeeds. Indeed, he doesn't even understand that what he's done is wrong. This would leave a very different impression. Moller explains: "Punishing a character by investing them with an awful insight into themselves might be effective because it's satisfying for us to know that the character realizes what they've done. Punishing a bewildered, ignorant wrongdoer is unsatisfying; what we want is that he *realize* how awful he's been, that he grasp our own point of view."[3]

Moller's insight is that what we really want when we demand justice is something that only the wrongdoer can give us. We want him to see himself *from our point of view* or to acknowledge our authority *vis-à-vis* himself. With this insight in mind, we can start to see what demanding justice and being subject to injustice have in common. Both involve our depending on the will of the wrongdoer. And this is a bad position to be in—not least because real-world villains seldom show the self-reflective moral discernment of their cinematic counterparts. Even if they did, though, we should want to get out of the relationship of dependence with the wrongdoer.

3. Dan Moller, "Anticipated Emotions and Emotional Valence," *Philosopher's Imprint* 11, no. 9 (July 2011): 15, https://tinyurl.com/hjyh6nyv. Italics original.

So much for plan A. We can't count on justice providing a satisfying end to the world, not so much because we can't count on justice but because we shouldn't expect justice to play the role in our lives that we want it to play. So, what about plan B? According to Charles, plan B involves giving up our demand for justice and instead adopting an attitude of mercy or kindness. I'm not sure what precisely the right label is, but the idea is that we should want to help out where we can. Charles uses the metaphor of a burning house. If you find you're in a burning house, the first thing you might want to do is get out yourself, to get as far away from it as you can. But having escaped, you might want to go back in and see if you can help others get out as well. (I'm not so sure I would want to go back in, but I can at least see that disposition as virtuous.)

Here's the important thing about the end of the world. If you can get yourself to abandon plan A and opt instead for plan B, that doesn't just make you more prepared for when the world ends. It reorients you toward the end of the world in a way that makes your current life better.

How can it affect how we live our lives now? The point, Charles suggested, was that once we have moved from plan A to plan B, we can live our lives without fear of needing to convince others that we're right all the time. We can even go a step further and learn from the ideas and traditions of those who are different from us. As an example, he offers his own religious practice. Charles has long been active in the local leadership of his Latter-day Saint congregation. He also followed the Buddhist practice of keeping a shrine to his ancestors. And he also had served in the Latter-day Saint temple to perform ordinances for those ancestors.

A Twist

Family home evening imposes a distinctive formality on family conversation. There's an official lesson, followed by a prayer and (hopefully) a game and (still more hopefully) a treat. After Charles finished his lesson, he opened the floor up to questions. A few polite queries followed, and Jen—a usually quiet, unfailingly considerate member of the family—raised her hand. Then something almost unprecedented—for any family home evening—happened. She posed an objection.

It went like this. In the official account of the First Vision, Joseph Smith asks his motivating question directly: "Who of all these parties are right; or, are they all wrong together?" (Joseph Smith—History [JSH] 1:10). Here is Joseph's retelling in the official (1838) version: "I was answered that I must join none of them, for they were all wrong; and the Personage who addressed me said that all their creeds were an abomination in his sight; that those professors were all corrupt, that: 'they draw near to me with their lips, but their hearts are far from me, they teach for doctrines the commandments of men, having a form of godliness, but they deny the power thereof'" (JSH 1:19).

Although Jen was careful to put the point in a more evenhanded, curious way, there was still a clear question here. It seemed like Charles was saying that Buddhist practice and teaching, and Latter-day Saint practice and teaching, were both true. Was he saying that other religions also could "be true"—whatever that amounted to exactly? And, if he was, how did that fit with the answer to Joseph's prayer: that no other religions were true.

Charles took the question in, turning his head at an angle as if to see it more clearly. "Well," he said, "I think Joseph got an answer to the question he asked." He paused for a moment. "Maybe, if he would have asked a different question, he would have gotten a different answer."

Chapter 9

Quietism

Charles's answer is an instance of what philosophers call quietism.[4] Here I am going to pause to introduce some technical terminology. And to talk about Harry Potter. I hope both will prove useful.

A quietist response to a question is a way of declining to answer or of refusing the question. Sometimes, it seems like the right answer to a yes-or-no question is neither yes nor no—that the question itself is somehow on the wrong track. It will help to have a case to work with. Recall the discussion between Harry Potter and Dumbledore at King's Cross. Moments before, Voldemort has struck Harry with a killing curse, and now Harry is reunited with his beloved mentor, whom we haven't seen since his own death almost an entire book earlier. They talk for the whole chapter. Here is how their conversation ends:

> He stood up, and Dumbledore did the same, and they looked for a long moment into each other's faces.
> "Tell me one last thing," said Harry, "Is this real? Or has this been happening inside my head?"
> Dumbledore beamed at him, and his voice sounded loud and strong in Harry's ears even though the bright mist was descending again, obscuring his figure.
> "Of course it is happening inside your head, Harry, but why on earth should that mean it is not real?"[5]

4. The view I discuss here differs from religious or ethical quietisms, which emphasize human passivity or nonresistance. Thanks to Derek Keefe for bringing this to my attention.

5. J. K. Rowling, *Harry Potter and the Deathly Hallows* (London: Arthur A. Levine Books, 2017).

J. K. Rowling would later describe this as her favorite line of the series, one she had waited for seven long books to write. Harry's question asks which of two things is true: has their conversation been real, or has it been in his head? Dumbledore's answer points out that the question itself might be misconceived: the fact that their conversation has taken place in Harry's head does not entail that it isn't real. Harry hadn't noticed that his question itself might be controverted, but that is what the response reveals. True to his usual style, Dumbledore makes no hard-and-fast assertions. He does not insist that their conversation has been real, only that its having taken place in Harry's head doesn't settle things one way or the other. In this way, his response refuses the question.

Now, let's take another classic example. Is morality real? The realist says, yes, morality is as real as the desk I'm writing on! The skeptic says, no, there is nothing real to morality—instead there are just moral attitudes people have and moral language that people use. But there is nothing over and above the attitudes and language. Morality, says the skeptic, is all inside your head.

Are these the only options? Gideon Rosen gives us an analogy. Consider what's funny. Is *the funny* real? We usually think of funniness as paradigmatically subjective, just in the head. Imagine an alien anthropologist comes down to Earth to study humans' sense of humor. The alien conducts extensive, rigorous research, and eventually figures out exactly which jokes we will find funny and when. The alien anthropologist can predict how the concept funny will be employed and which things will—and which things won't—be judged funny.[6]

6. Gideon Rosen, "Objectivity and Modern Idealism: What Is the Question?," in *Philosophy in Mind: The Place of Philosophy in the Study of Mind*, ed. Michaelis Michael and John O'Leary-Hawthorne, Philosophical Studies Series (Dordrecht: Springer Netherlands, 1994), 302.

Now, the question is, Is what's funny real or not? Of course, it's true that funniness is in our heads in the sense that it is a human phenomenon supervening on human minds, but that was also uncontroversially true of morality. From the alien anthropologist's viewpoint, the funny is a phenomenon that is observable, that has patterns that can be investigated and reported, and about which predictions extending reliably into the future can be made. In other words, what is funny looks as real and objective as anything could be, its being "all in our minds" notwithstanding. Here is how Rosen sums it up:

> The problem was to draw a notional line between objective features of the world and those which the mind somehow constructs. This contrast is introduced to us by a series of metaphors which are most at home in a Kantian framework where the Mind's relation to the world of experience is problematic. The question was, what are we to make of the metaphors once this metaphysics gives way to a naturalism according to which the only minds there are are *parts* of the natural world itself? . . . In each case I suggested that the initial promise depends on a subtle conflation: a contrast drawn at the level of properties or facts. But this move is always illegitimate without further argument, and we saw some reason to think that in these cases the argument cannot be available.[7]

In other words, to ask whether something is real or is in our minds supposes that there is a sharp difference between the two. But, of course, it is hard to say that our minds are not, themselves, among the things in the world. Like Harry, the realist wanted a firm distinction between these things, but

7. Rosen, "Objectivity and Modern Idealism," 313-14.

maybe no such distinction is forthcoming. Perhaps we could grant the metaphysical picture that the moral subjectivist advances but then say that, even conceding the subjectivist's stylized facts, morality remains as real as it ever could have been.[8] Like Dumbledore, the moral quietist responds to the question of whether morality is real or in our heads by refusing the question. Of course it's in our heads, Rosen is saying, but why ever should that mean it isn't real?

Family Home Evening, Again

Back to Charles's answer. Joseph had asked God which of all the churches is true. None of them is the answer he gets. Does that mean Charles's Buddhism and Mormonism must be in tension in some way? Charles gives a quietist answer, or one that poses a challenge back to the question. Maybe it was something about what Joseph asked that made him get the answer he got.

Recall the other quietist responses. "Is this real, or in my mind?" asks Harry. Dumbledore refuses the question by pointing out that Harry is assuming the premise that it isn't both real *and* in his mind. But Harry's suppressed premise might be false. "Is morality real, or is it just in the minds of humans?" philosophers have wondered. Gideon Rosen's reply is similar. The philosophical debate has been assuming that if morality was all in people's minds, then it wasn't real. But that premise could be wrong. Morality could both be in the mind and objectively real.

Joseph Smith asked, "Who of all these parties are right; or, are they all wrong together?" (JSH 1:10). It might be that the

8. Is it a fudge to say "it ever could have been"? Well, morality might still not be as real as some things. See Crispin Wright, *Truth and Objectivity* (Cambridge, MA: Harvard University Press, 1993).

question itself contains a premise that could be worth scrutinizing. Perhaps it is not the case that one—and only one—among the competing religionists is right, and yet also not the case that they are all wrong together.

This might sound like a contradiction, but let's not give up without trying. Let's assume, with Joseph Smith as well as his Christian contemporaries, that there is one God. Does it follow that there must be one religion that uniquely expresses the truth about God? Maybe not. Imagine, for example, two different groups of humans with very different conceptual maps. Psychologists and philosophers since at least Kant have appreciated that sometimes our concepts can affect the kinds of experiences we have.[9] Very roughly, this is because our emotion concepts, and even our sensory concepts, are more finely grained than our physical experiences. Say, for example, that you are experiencing a sudden increase in your heartbeat, a dryness in your mouth, and a feeling that your cheeks are flushed. Are you afraid, excited, nervous, anxious, or some combination? The fact about what you're feeling isn't settled by the sensory facts alone. It matters what context you're in and how it makes sense for you to interpret things in that context. What concepts make sense for you to apply to the experience you're having?—this is the crucial question.

Now, consider two people who have very different religious experiences. A woman whose son is fighting in World War II reports seeing a vision of Mary, who offers her assurance and instruction.[10] A sailor in World War II fears his ship is going to capsize in heavy weather and prays for divine protection. In response, he receives a spiritual instruction to investigate

9. See Lisa Feldman Barrett, *How Emotions Are Made: The Secret Life of the Brain* (Boston: Mariner Books, 2017).

10. Robert A. Orsi, *History and Presence* (2016; reprint, Cambridge, MA: The Belknap Press of Harvard University Press, 2018).

the ship's engines himself.[11] The first person is a Catholic, and the second is a Latter-day Saint. Their respective experiences might surprise members of the other group. Latter-day Saints don't typically see Marian visions. Catholics might not expect a providential to-do list. These are relatively simple examples. When you think of all that goes into experiences of God—the feelings, beliefs, words (heard, felt, or exchanged)—it would be surprising if there wasn't considerable variation in what believers experience.

The theologian John Hick has suggested that we might think of all of our different experiences as arising from the same God but refracted very differently through our own conceptual prisms. Hick puts it this way: "The Gods, then, are phenomenal appearances of the Real existing, with their omni- and other properties, in the thought of the worshipping community. But in praying to them we may in fact (unknown to us) be in contact with a real personal presence which is an 'angel,' in the sense of an intermediate being between ourselves and the Real, corresponding to the angels, archangels of the western monotheisms, or devas (gods with a small g) of Indian religion, or the heavenly Buddhas of one interpretation of one strand of Mahayan Buddhism."[12]

This might not be exactly clear. Kind of like Gideon Rosen and Dumbledore, Hick is thinking about how religious experience could be both real *and* in our minds. Hick's idea is to contrast our experience of God—or God's phenomenal ap-

---

11. Larry Y. Wilson, "Take the Holy Spirit as Your Guide" (talk, general conference of the Church of Jesus Christ of Latter-day Saints, Salt Lake City, Utah, April 1, 2018), accessed March 13, 2023, https://tinyurl.com /t2p7f8t3.

12. John Hick, "Response to Hasker," in *Evidence and Religious Belief*, ed. Kelly James Clark and Raymond J. VanArragon (Oxford: Oxford University Press, 2011), 200; quoted in Daniel Howard-Snyder, "Who or What Is God, according to John Hick?," *Topoi* 36, no. 4 (Dec. 2017): 571–86, https://tinyurl .com/2catxrpz.

pearance—with the reality that underlies that experience. Our spiritual experiences might really be traceable to God, but this phenomenal appearance (the God we perceive) is a kind of intermediate figure between us and God. Call it an angel, or a vision, or a heavenly Buddha. But whatever you want to call it, God must enter our mind through our own sensory experience, as shaped with our own concepts.

What's important about Hick's idea is that it offers a way of explaining religious disagreement—and also of explaining it away.[13] We inevitably have to use the concepts we have to describe God, and these concepts figure both in the initial shaping of our experiences and in our subsequent expression of those experiences to others. Because we are limited to talking about our own, private experiences of God using the tools afforded by our own community's concepts, it shouldn't surprise us if much of what we say conflicts with what other people say. But such conflicts may admit of a kind of deeper reconciliation. The philosopher Christine Korsgaard asks us to imagine encountering an alien who hears, rather than sees, the color green.[14] Imagine that it just so happens that when light in the relevant wavelength reaches the alien, they experience a dull buzzing sound rather than the color green. One spring day you're walking with the alien, and you come across a giant oak tree whose leaves have just come out. "What a beautiful green tree!" you say. "What a strong buzzing noise it makes," the alien says.

---

13. For another appreciative response to theological difference, see John J. Thatamanil, *Circling the Elephant: A Comparative Theology of Religious Diversity* (New York: Fordham University Press, 2020); Lesslie Newbigin, *The Gospel in a Pluralist Society* (Grand Rapids: Eerdmans, 1989).

14. See Christine M. Korsgaard, "Realism and Constructivism in Twentieth-Century Moral Philosophy," in "Philosophy in America at the Turn of the Century," ed. Robert Audi, supplement, *Journal of Philosophical Research* 28 (October 2003): 99–122, https://tinyurl.com/33mmxvcf.

If you didn't know the background, it would be easy to think you were disagreeing. "Who is right about the tree?" an on-looker might demand, "or are they both wrong together?" But once you know the background story, this no longer looks like the best way of putting the question. You can work out something approximating a translation between your experience and the alien's. You are responding to the same thing but with different experiences and concepts. On Hick's account, religion is something like that. We think we're disagreeing, but that disagreement might be a product of our experiential differences and conceptual limitations.

Now we can put a more developed quietist challenge to Joseph Smith's question to God. It's not the case that one religion was right, but it's also not exactly true that they were all wrong together. Rather, they (or at least some of them) were probably expressing their experiences of God as best they could with the conceptual tools they had available. Joseph's question, like Harry's and like the moral realist's, contained a premise that could be wrong.

Joseph Smith and the Restoration

Someone might object that I've played too fast and loose with the original objection. Didn't God *tell* Joseph that all of the other religions were false? If there was something amiss with Joseph's question, why does God seem to answer it so directly?

I'll come back to this, but first I want to think about the details of Smith's accounts of his experience. In his earliest (1832) account of his first vision, he explains that as a twelve- or fifteen-year-old, he studied the Bible and came to the conclusion that none of the contending Christian churches had the truth. "My mind became exceedingly distressed, for I became convicted of my sins, and by searching the scriptures I found that mankind did not come unto the Lord but that they had apostatized from the true and living faith, and there was no society or denomination that was built upon the gospel of Jesus Christ as recorded in the New Testament."[15] Later, in the 1835 account of his experience, Smith quotes Matthew 7:7 and James 1:5, from which he infers that God will answer prayers directly. He doesn't describe studying these verses, but they come to his mind. He prays for (and receives) forgiveness for his sins.[16] Only in the 1838 version is his judgment of other churches a product of God's directly addressing the issue rather than of his own interpretation of the scriptural text. Ann Taves reads Smith's various accounts as suggesting that he first concluded, based on his reading of scriptures as a teenager, that no church was true. Later, observing persistent disagreement about scriptural interpretation, the twentysomething Joseph Smith came to "regard the exegetical method as unreliable."[17] In the 1838 version, he held that "teachers of religion" read the same passages so differently as to "destroy all confidence in settling the question over an appeal to the Bible."[18] So, he gave up on one method (solving disagreement through interpretation) and came to rely on another (solving disagreement through divine communication).

15. Joseph Smith, history, circa summer 1832, p. 2, Joseph Smith Papers, Church History Library, Salt Lake City, UT, accessed March 13, 2023, https://tinyurl.com/4eudkkcz. Grammar, punctuation, and capitalization have been regularized.

16. Joseph Smith, journal, 1835–1836, p. 23, Joseph Smith Papers, Church History Library, Salt Lake City, UT, accessed February 16, 2023, https://tinyurl.com/mr246x8z.

17. Ann Taves, *Revelatory Events: Three Case Studies of the Emergence of New Spiritual Paths* (Princeton: Princeton University Press, 2016), 77.

18. Joseph Smith, history, circa June 1839–circa 1841 [draft 2], p. 2, Joseph Smith Papers, Church History Library, Salt Lake City, UT, accessed March 13, 2023, https://tinyurl.com/3h7dn2fk.

And even in the 1838 account the personage does not precisely say that the other churches are false. Not to quibble too much, but Smith is never given some set of propositions, believed by other churches, that are not true. Instead, he's told that "their creeds were an abomination" to God. He would maintain his negative attitude toward creeds throughout his life. However, his complaints had less to do with their doctrinal content than with their effects on individual worship. He even allowed that "all of them had some truth." Still, he could not subscribe to them because they "set up stakes and say hitherto shalt thou come and no further."[19] The problem with creeds is that they grant official imprimatur to some particular resolution of a scriptural question and thereby discourage individuals from seeking out their own answers. But Smith thought individuals had to seek out God for themselves—that was the best and most important method! It's even OK if that meant getting things wrong sometimes. "Methodists have creeds which a man must believe or be kicked out of the church. I want the liberty of believing as I please, it feels so good not to be trammeled. It don't prove that a man is not a good man, because he errs in doctrine."[20]

In his objections, Smith sounds almost Emersonian. (Emerson himself hated creeds on the grounds that they encouraged conformity and undercut a person's self-reliance.)[21] Smith's own

19. Joseph Smith, discourse, October 15, 1843, as reported by Willard Richards, p. 129, Joseph Smith Papers, Church History Library, Salt Lake City, UT, accessed February 16, 2023, https://tinyurl.com/4yp395hz.

20. Joseph Smith, discourse, April 8, 1843, as reported by William Clayton-B, p. 2, Joseph Smith Papers, Church History Library, Salt Lake City, UT, accessed February 16, 2023, https://tinyurl.com/y5z45jks.

21. If you want the detailed comparison, see Ryan W. Davis, "Frontier Kantianism: Autonomy and Authority in Ralph Waldo Emerson and Joseph Smith," *Journal of Religious Ethics* 46, no. 2 (2018): 332–59, https://tinyurl.com/2s4j4v7w.

anticreedalism also offers an interpretive lens on the divine personage's initial warning that creeds were an "abomination." In the Gospel of Mark's little apocalypse, Jesus warns of a coming "abomination of desolation," to be found "standing where it ought not" (13:14). Mark then makes a parenthetical aside, "let him that readeth understand." Mark's oblique reference is to Daniel's prophecy of an image of Zeus profaning the temple (Daniel 8:13; 11:31). God vacates the temple after it's desecrated by idols. The abomination is that the temple is desolate of the divine presence. The personage who speaks to Smith repurposes the concept in warning about creeds. How could creeds be an "abomination"? Smith's much-later statements against creeds make sense of one possibility. Creeds foreclose the need for individual communion with God. They set up stakes that leave the individual outside the divine presence. Like the abomination that leaves the temple desolate, creeds leave the individual believer desolate of God's active involvement in shaping their own beliefs.

From his earliest accounts of his first vision, Joseph Smith is distressed by human wickedness. The wickedness foremost on his mind was religious strife. The "war of words and tumult of opinions" made him wonder what was "to be done" (JSH 1:10). Later in life, he proposed what he called the "grand fundamental principle of Mormonism," according to which the Saints ought to "embrace all truth, let it come from where it may."[22] He had explicitly in mind other religions ("Presbyterian, Methodist, Baptist"), admonishing "get all the good in the world, come out a pure Mormon."[23] Don't worry that taking on truths from other

22. Joseph Smith, discourse, July 9, 1843, as reported by Willard Richards, p. 302, Joseph Smith Papers, Church History Library, Salt Lake City, UT, accessed February 17, 2023, https://tinyurl.com/vxz5uyah.

23. Joseph Smith, journal, December 1842–June 1844; book 3, July 15, 1843–February 29, 1844, p. 14, Joseph Smith Papers, Church History

religions could dilute Mormonism! If receiving and embracing truths from any source just *is* Mormonism's fundamental principle—the principle at the foundation of all the other doctrines Mormonism avows—then accepting any other religion's truths would be an expression, rather than a violation, of a believer's specifically Mormon devotion. Smith elsewhere described "friendship" as Mormonism's grand fundamental principle, leading some commentators to hold that there were two grand fundamental principles.[24] My own preferred reading is that embracing the truths one finds in another is just what friendship is about. On this reading, there is only one grand fundamental principle (after all, with its auspicious title, how many can there be?), but it can be described in two different ways.

Ending the War

Let's take stock. As a young man, Joseph Smith was deeply upset by Christians fighting each other with words. He was so concerned that he came to despair whether Jesus's ancient faith was on the Earth at all. Perhaps he also came to doubt whether questions could be resolved by appealing to disputed scriptural texts. He became convinced that individuals had to go to God directly. In his own first vision of God, he was told by a divine personage that religious leaders were corrupt, that "they teach for doctrine the commandments of men, having a form of godliness, but they deny the power thereof." The divine presence was not found anywhere in the war of words that Smith saw, and its

---

Library, Salt Lake City, UT, accessed February 17, 2023, https://tinyurl.com/ywcpm4as.

24. Don Bradley, "'The Grand Fundamental Principles of Mormonism': Joseph Smith's Unfinished Reformation," *Sunstone*, April 2006, 32–41.

absence was an abomination. From this quoted passage, he infers about the churches that "they were all wrong" (JSH 1:19).

My own interpretation of Smith's various accounts of his experience places the war of words among Christians as a central problem. Like the villains in Matthew's trilogy of parables about authority (Matthew 21-22), the problem is that if leaders of religious groups are worried about fighting each other, they are not attentive enough to cooperate with God. And if they are not choosing to cooperate with God, then they are on their own, desolate of God's presence.

What is the right way of responding to a war of words? Throughout his life, Smith was deeply concerned with finding a language that would somehow transcend disagreement, a language whose concepts and meaning would be universally accessible.[25] That aspiration will have to wait for the eschaton. In the meanwhile, Joseph Smith wanted to build Zion. He hoped that the pure in heart would be pure Mormons—that is, they would be willing to understand and accept the insights of others. Even his language for pure Mormonism comes close to the language of Zion—where all would be of one heart and one mind. On one occasion, he gives the grand fundamental principle in terms of "receiving" what's "truth."[26] On another, he formulates it in terms of "embracing" what's "good."[27] Even his two locutions for how to unify with other traditions keep the Zion-building structure of oneness in mental content and content of the heart.

How can the war of words be brought to an end? One way would be to win the war outright, a kind of theological version

25. Samuel Morris Brown, *Joseph Smith's Translation: The Words and Worlds of Early Mormonism* (New York: Oxford University Press, 2020).

26. Smith, discourse, July 9, 1843, as reported by Willard Richards, p. 302.

27. Smith, journal, December 1842-June 1844; book 3, July 15, 1843-February 29, 1844, p. 14.

of the Roman "peace through victory."²⁸ But the problem with this is that there is no reason to think that even the unmediated divine truth, if one could possess it with God's own concepts and express it in God's own language, would prevail. Such truth would be just as eligible for other humans to disagree with and fight over as any other assertion.

There is another way to envision a detente in the war of words. Call it "peace through friendship" or maybe "peace through neighbor love." This is by ceasing from trying to win an argument and instead engaging with others according to some different principle. It would be to take the end of the world, plan B.

If we do that, how should we read Joseph Smith's question, "Who of all these parties are right; or, are they all wrong together?" My suggestion is that it is no dishonor to his intention to read the question as limited, as the question of a wonderer who doesn't yet know how to formulate the question he feels. It is part of Smith's own story that he was distressed by the conflict and that he was brought low by thoughts of his own need for forgiveness. It shouldn't surprise us, then, if his question was the question of someone who saw the religious conflicts through a glass darkly, with the concepts that were not quite right for the job. The question takes for granted that the only way out of the war is peace through victory. Either one side is right and has secured victory, or nobody is right, and someone else needs to come in and secure victory. Joseph Smith, in that moment, was thinking about the war of words in the same way all the other combatants were thinking about it. What those combatants had in common, according to Smith's restorationist religion, was a lack of access to God directly. In that way, his

28. John Dominic Crossan, *How to Read the Bible and Still Be a Christian: Is God Violent? An Exploration from Genesis to Revelation* (San Francisco: HarperOne, 2016).

own question is better understood within his tradition as the last moment of the apostasy rather than as the first moment of the restoration. Given his belief that God's active participation is needed to escape apostasy, this is exactly what we should expect of the moment before God's speaking begins.

Conclusion

A few years ago, I was eating dinner with Charles and his family. He commented that we would understand the scriptures differently if we had grown up on a farm.

"What do you mean?" I asked him.

"Think about when Jesus talks about sheep," he said. "Remember that one sheep who leaves the other ninety-nine and heads up to the mountains?"

"Yeah, I remember," I said.

After a moment, he went on, "Nowadays we've bred sheep to be dumb. But when Jesus was alive, sheep had to be smart. They had to be smart if they were going to survive." He paused for a moment and looked out the window onto Center Street in Provo. "If we understood that, we'd probably think about the scriptures differently."

I expected that he was going to say the different thing that we might think. I waited for a moment for him to settle back to the question.

"Anyway," he said, "how has fishing been around here?"

I countered, "Wait, wait—first tell me the different thing we would think."

Charles shrugged as if he didn't really want to. But then he sighed obligingly. "We'd probably think whatever that one sheep was doing, it probably had a good reason."

CHAPTER 10

The Legend of Quint McCallister

"We've got a point." My dad's voice was taut, his whisper urgent, as if he were shouting under his breath. When he was hunting, his voice sounded alive.

I was eight years old—just old enough (according to my parents) to be carrying a shotgun rather than the BB gun with which I had pursued sparrows in the undergrowth in other years. This was the moment we had prepared for. In the long months between hunting seasons, my parents would sit on the living room couch, shotgun in hand. They'd practice shouldering it against a flock of ducks flying over the porch at last light. Sometimes, just the presence of the shotgun would remind them of a story. The time my mom rolled down a desert hill out past Kingman to get away from an aggressive bull. A story when my dad had tracked pheasants in the fresh snow. Every nick on Mom's Winchester side-by-side, "Bobo," called to mind some story or other. Mom wanted Dad's gun to have a name as well, but he wasn't interested. However, he couldn't stop himself from trading off with her in retelling the details of some hunt or other from the times before I was born. One of them would remember some detail, and rehearsing it would prompt the other with the next piece of the narrative. They'd work their way to the story's completion, usually some comedically unanticipated mishap. Failure in hunting is the norm. Storytelling must accommodate that fact.

Dad whistled to get my attention. He was gesturing to make sure I saw the black-and-gray dog some seventy yards above us. Cholla, our wirehaired pointer, had located a covey of quail. He was perfectly frozen, facing up a shallow draw, flanked on either side by grassy ridges with a few oak trees mixed in. Cholla was young enough that he would sometimes mistakenly point rabbits or small birds, but this time his statue-like stillness revealed confidence. The quail were right in front of him.

My dad had rehearsed this moment a hundred times. Rule #3: Close the distance. Don't stop walking. Don't look for the birds on the ground. Just get to the dog. The closer you are to the dog, the better your chances. The flush of a covey of quail takes only fractions of a second. My dad had cared about school and work, but this was the moment he lived for. He skirted around to my right, signaling at Mom to take up a position on the ridge above me and to my left. Rule #2: Cover the angles. Dad wanted everyone to be positioned so that whichever way the birds flushed, someone would have a shot. Rule #1: Always shoot.

I advanced toward Cholla, my hands sweaty against the old 20 gauge's engraved receiver. The drumming of my heart drowned out the wind in the trees and the rustle of grass under my boots. I came even with the dog's nose. I scanned the ground below me. Everything was perfectly still. "Nothing!" I said.

"They're here," Dad countered, breathless.

"Cholla's pointing right at a rock," I insisted.

"Kick it." I glanced at my father, some ten yards above me on the ridge. He nodded.

I obliged, rolling the side of my boot into the granite stone protruding from the grass. In a burst of color and sound, some twelve quail erupted from the grass around my feet. They filled the sky. The 20 gauge was on my shoulder, tracking to my right up the ridge. As the gun moved, my eyes down the barrel caught Dad's old orange cap. My swing faded. The quail were already evaporating into the oaks, settling into the grass somewhere up on the hillside.

"What was that!" Dad demanded. This was the one thing over which he ever expressed frustration. I knew even before he spoke (which is to say, before any time had passed at all). He looked at me with incomprehension. "There were so many!"

"They were headed your way," I offered, truthfully.

"You've gotta shoot," he said. "It's fine if you miss, but you have to shoot. I won't say a word against you for missing." It was true. I had never received anything but encouragement after a missed shot.

"Well . . ." I started, my voice inflecting upward.

Dad waved me off. "Shoot first, and ask questions later." He said that all the time, never ironically. Unless everything he said was a little ironic. In any case, I could tell my deliberate consideration of the moment was not to his taste.

"I was just worried I might hit you," I apologized.

"You're not gonna hit me."

"How do you know?"

"You're not gonna hit me."

1

My father is a storyteller. When I was growing up, our small town in rural Arizona had two, and then finally three Latter-day Saint congregations, with a few others collecting scattered homesteads and a few ranches to the north and south of our town. I don't think it's an exaggeration to say that by the time I was in high school, my dad was one of the most beloved church speakers between the Mogollon Rim and Tonto Basin. His secret, I think, is that he told stories for *the story*. There's a common temptation to press stories into having a point. Dad told stories that he wanted to tell, points be damned.

Dad told the story of Quint McCallister as part of a talk in church. I was around sixteen or seventeen. The story is set in at the fictional McCallister ranch in the Big Hole River Valley just outside of Wisdom, Montana, one of my family's favored vacation spots when I was young. Quint is the youngest child in his family. By the time of the story, his four sisters have grown up and moved away, leaving him with greater responsibilities to shoulder around the ranch.

Each summer, the ranches all through the Big Hole region had to decide how much hay to put up for the winter. I am far enough removed from my father's own ranching childhood and adolescence that the details of this process are obscure to me. But the idea in the story is that the rancher faces a kind of dilemma. If the winter will be long and hard, then it is important to put a lot of hay in store. However, if the winter will be mild, then prudence recommends setting less aside. The problem is, How can you predict in the waning days of summer how hard the winter will be? Each year, Quint is impressed that his dad manages to get the answer roughly right, even though no one seems to know what the winter will be like when the days are still long and the valley floor is still green.

Reaching the age where he needed to figure out how things work, Quint inquires of his dad how he knows how many hay bales to set aside for the winter. His father tells him the answer is simple. A few miles from the McCallister ranch, up toward the Beartooth Mountains, is a local chief of a Blackfoot village his father knows. Each summer, the Blackfoot tan deer and elk hides in anticipation of the winter. If they tanned only a few hides, it meant they anticipated a mild winter. But if they tanned many hides, it was because they expected the winter to be severe. As far as he could remember, Quint's father knew the Blackfoot chief to be better at forecasting the coming winter than any other source in the valley. So, if the Blackfoot tanned many hides, he took in many hay bales. And if they tanned only a few, he set aside less hay for winter.

Of course, this answer just pushes things back a step. What Quint really wanted to know was how to tell whether the winter would be hard. He already knew that someone knew the answer, since his dad did. But he didn't just want to know that someone knew; he wanted to know something like the real story—what explained how you could predict the winter's expected duration.

Once he knew that the Blackfoot chief possessed this knowledge, Quint wanted to get to the bottom of things. But for several years, his father told him he wasn't old enough to go bothering anyone about it. Finally, a summer day comes when, like all the days before, Quint finishes his chores around the ranch and again asks his dad if this year he can go inquire how the chief knows how hard the winter will be. This time he decides he will insist on going. After all, he will one day have to take more responsibility for running the ranch. He needs to know how to make decisions.

To his surprise, Quint's father agrees that he should go up to see the chief. However, his father demurs from going with him. His arthritis is bothering him, he says, and it's a considerable ride up to the village. So, Quint sets off alone through the valley, passing by the haystacks along either bank of the meandering river. The real-life Big Hole area is still sometimes called the Valley of Ten Thousand Stacks. (Or so I'm told.) Arriving at the village, he asks for the chief and is invited to take a seat next to an older man. He introduces himself, and the chief asks about his father. Quint excuses his absence, explaining that he can't ride as much as he used to. The chief nods. "We are old men now," he says.

To me, "We are old men now" is the most poignant line in the story. I imagine Quint realizing something then that he might not have put together before. This older man knew his father as a person, and his father must have known him as well. More than that, the chief's suggestion that they were old seemed to carry a meaning beyond what was spoken. It suggested that the chief remembered not only a time when he was young but a time when Quint's father had been young too. He and Quint's father had been young together. Sometime in the past, they had lived the lives of young men. Perhaps they had traveled the Big Hole country by horse together?

But that is not what Quint asks. With a gesture to the hides being tanned around them, he asks about planning for winter. "How can you tell how the winter will be? My father says you are a wise man."

The chief considers Quint and responds, "Help me up." The boy offers the older man a hand, and they walk to a ledge overlooking the valley below. "What do you see?" the chief asks. "The Big Hole," Quint responds, gesturing to the region's most notable feature. The chief presses, "What else?" "My family's ranch?" comes the reply. "What else?" Quint surveys the valley from the clear mountain air. "I see thousands of haystacks."

This response satisfies the chief. Each summer, he then explains, when the days start to get shorter and the crisp hint of fall is in the air, he looks down into the valley to the McCallister ranch. If McCallister puts up only a few haystacks, then that means he anticipates a mild winter. In that case, the Blackfoot would tan only a few hides. But if McCallister puts up many haystacks, the winter will be hard, and the Blackfoot prepared by tanning many hides.

That's the end of the story. However, as is sometimes the case with parables, there is another story that goes with it. Most people think that when parables are told together, the pairing itself can help with the interpretation. I think that might be true in this case, and so I'm going to rehearse the next story from my dad's talk.

This story is about my dad's dog, a German wirehaired pointer named Cholla. (When he had been in college, my dad's best friend had a dog named Sage, after the primary flora of the Wyoming range they hunted together. Keeping the tradition, my dad named his dog after a cactus distinctive to the Sonoran Desert, the primary quail habitat south of our family home.) Though Cholla grew up hunting quail in the Arizona sun, his thick, brushy hair was not especially well-suited to the climate. Drahthaars like Cholla were bred to hunt in the Northern European winter, not in the desert heat. I have many memories of Cholla—panting—walking back to my father to take a long drink from the canteen that Dad carried just for him.

One day, however, my dad and Cholla were hunting at a work colleague's ranch on one side or other of the Arizona-Mexico border. (Apparently, there was a time when the boundary was not so clearly demarcated.) The very southern tip of Arizona, and the northern part of Sonora below it, consist in relatively high-elevation rolling grasslands and oak-covered hills. It's not uncommon for snowstorms to blow through mountains during winter quail hunts. My dad and his colleague—a large, jovial oilman nicknamed Tank—were hunting on one such blustery winter day. Scenting conditions were ideal for Cholla, and he found one covey of quail after another. I should underscore that this day is literally the stuff of legend. I am not sure how many times I have heard this story, but it must be among the two or three most retold hunting stories in my household (where hunting stories are a nontrivial part of the total communication).

About an hour into the hunt, Tank asks my dad what he would take for the dog. "Not for sale," my dad replies. Tank counters that everything is for sale. My dad offers, "A million bucks." They laugh it off and keep hunting. Cholla continues to hunt with an exhibition level of precision. After a while Tank says again, "I'll give you $2,000 for that dog." My dad counters that this sum would work out to about a dollar for every hour he had spent training him. Tank agrees and offers $3,000. A little while later, he offers $5,000. Dad responds by saying, "The dog is not worth that, and, even if he was, I could not explain to the kids why I had taken money for their dog." But then in the talk, he goes on to say something he doesn't say in his exchange with Tank: "Truth was I loved the dog and had no intention of selling him at any price—that is, unless it was a million dollars."

He then goes on to mention another time, when the bishop of our congregation was visiting our house. He was—as was common at that time and place—dressed in camouflage hunting gear. A medical doctor, the radio he carried went off as he was walking up to our porch. Startled, Cholla got agitated and bit him. (At this point in the story, he says he didn't mention that it took him months to train the dog to bite bishops.) Unlike in the story of Quint McCallister, Dad ends this story by saying its point: "Now, as much as I love the dog, I cannot completely trust him."

3

Let's go back to the exchange between Quint and the Blackfoot chief. The story ends with a twist—and however much one might see that twist coming, it seems to me that it's not altogether clear what to make of it. The whole story sets up the expectation that the chief holds some secret knowledge. McCallister's secret is that he knows the chief knows how to predict the winter. And, in fact, the chief does know how to predict the winter, and so he *does* take himself to be in possession of a secret. He knows McCallister knows how to predict the winter. And as Quint and the reader already know, he's right about that too. McCallister does have a good track record of getting it right. The twist is it's hard to square how the secrets make sense together. McCallister can't, it seems, take a clue from the chief that the chief, in turn, takes from McCallister. It can't be secrets all the way down.

One way of putting the problem is that at some point, someone must have some access to the truth of the matter. If the old men have nothing but each other to go on, then neither has any access to the facts about the weather. The whole thing has no real, independent evidence at the bottom of it. In other words, both of their beliefs will look arbitrary with respect to the truth.

Here's an example. Suppose I ask you for directions to the building on campus I'm looking for, you point confidently to your left, and I start off in that direction. So far, it feels reasonable for me to think I know where I'm going. But suppose, for some reason, you had just decided before seeing me to flip a coin: if the coin came up heads, you resolved to give the next passerby correct directions. If the coin came up tails, you would point in exactly the wrong way. (Trust me—this is just how philosophy examples work. I'm not saying this would be a fun game.) Anyway, imagine that just as I'm arriving, you flip the coin. After glancing at the outcome, you politely (or, mischievously?) offer me directions.

What should we now think about my confidence that I know where I'm going? Of course, whether the coin comes up heads or tails has nothing to do with where the building is. So, if that is what determines how you give me directions, then it seems like your instruction—and, hence, my belief—is subject to an influence that is arbitrary with respect to the truth. If I knew you were playing this game, the smart thing to do would be to think that the odds I'm headed the right way are no better than chance. Because of the arbitrary influence, it turns out that my belief is unjustified.

Philosophers have worried about this sort of thing. John Stuart Mill observed that the Anglicans he lived around were typically very confident of their religious views. For the most part, the religious beliefs about which they were confident were those they had been raised with since childhood. But Mill noticed that the same was true of people in other religious traditions as well. He thought this was something that should give pause to his confident religious neighbors.

> In proportion to a man's want of confidence in his own soli-
> tary judgement, does he usually repose, with implicit trust,
> on the infallibility of "the world" in general. And the world,
> to each individual, means the part of it with which he comes
> in contact; his party, his sect, his church, his class of society:
> the man may be called, by comparison, almost liberal and
> large-minded to whom it means anything so comprehensive
> as his own country or his own age. Nor is his faith in this
> collective authority at all shaken by his being aware that
> other ages, countries, sects, churches, classes, and parties
> have thought, and even now think, the exact reverse. He de-
> volves upon his own world the responsibility of being in the
> right against the dissentient worlds of other people; and it
> never troubles him that mere accident has decided which of
> these numerous worlds is the object of his reliance, and that
> the same causes which make him a Churchman in London,
> would have made him a Buddhist or a Confucian in Pekin
> [Beijing].[1]

1. John Stuart Mill, *On Liberty, Utilitarianism and Other Essays*, ed. Mark

Mill's idea is that while the London churchman is confident that his Anglican Christianity is true, his confidence is no greater than that of the Buddhist in China in his respective tradition. What's more, pretty much all of the religious folks in London (as in China) grow up to share the religious views they were raised with. Unless he has some reason for thinking he's exceptional, the London churchman has to admit that if by chance he had been born in China, he would probably be just as confident of Buddhism as he now is in his Christianity. That can feel like an unnerving thought. The central claims of a religion—concerning whether there is some divine being or presence and, if so, what that being or presence is like—almost certainly don't have anything to do with whether you're born in London, Beijing, or the Big Hole River Valley. Presumably, where you are born is completely arbitrary with respect to the truths about God and the ultimate nature of reality. And for the reasons given already, if your beliefs are influenced by arbitrary causes, that sounds like bad news.[2]

4

When I heard my dad's talk in church, my reaction was that in the end, neither McCallister nor the old chief had any secrets about the winter. If Quint experienced any disappointment, it's never revealed. We are simply given the chief's final line: "If McCallister puts up little hay, the Blackfeet tan few hides, for

Philp and Frederick Rosen, 2nd ed. (Oxford: Oxford University Press, 2015), 20.

2. For a defense of religious belief, also originating from the Latter-day Saint tradition, see Terryl Givens and Nathaniel Givens, *Into the Headwinds: Why Belief Has Always Been Hard—and Still Is* (Grand Rapids: Eerdmans, 2022).

the winter will be easy." And that is the end. We don't see the expression on Quint's face as he hears the answer. Dad gives no editorial commentary about the story. The next line after the story is a quote by Joseph B. Wirthlin, a leader of the church at the time: "Integrity means always doing what is right and good, regardless of the immediate consequences."

Maybe Quint's father knew all along that there was no secret about how to predict the winter. Maybe the only secret was the joke he and the old chief had played on his son. Or maybe he regarded the question with a kind of wry humor. Perhaps there was a secret winter-forecasting system, or perhaps not, but he had reached a point where it made the most sense to consider the entire thing with a shrug. He had his way of doing things, and that was enough. Integrity might be about staying with the traditions you have, even when you find out they aren't the uniquely rational traditions you might have once imagined them to be.[3]

5

Though he always attended church, my dad was never much interested in arguing about religion. "Not everything means

---

3. Tim McKuen points out to me that this paragraph gives short shrift to the thought that along with accepting one's own tradition, it's good to remain open to finding truth in other traditions as well—especially after admitting the reality of one's own current epistemic limitations. How could a person maintain the stability of their own tradition alongside an openness to others? All I can do in this footnote is admit that the answer here is not enough. Tim's point is that remaining in one's own tradition— with its biases—seems to admit that one's perspective will always diverge from God's, and that accepting this difference nonchalantly might be something that concerns us.

something to me," he would say. "It means something to God," he agreed. "But it doesn't always mean something to me."

A few years ago, I asked him if he remembered the story of Quint McCallister. He descended the stairs and returned a few minutes later, a copy of the talk in his hand. I wanted to have another look at the text. Maybe McCallister's looking up at his old friend for answers wasn't the only rational thing to do, but maybe it wasn't a rational error either. Perhaps I felt like Quint should have been disappointed by the chief's answer because I had been expecting too much.

Let's go back for a moment to the London churchman and Mill's worry that beliefs formed under arbitrary influences couldn't be trusted. The churchman notices that if he had been born in China, he likely wouldn't accept any of his current religious views. And that is unsettling, because it seems like where he was born is irrelevant to the issue of what he should believe. So, if he is believing something for reasons irrelevant to its truth, then that sounds like bad news. It sounds like a wordy way of saying he was just guessing. It's like the universe flipped a coin before giving him religious directions, and he had no way of figuring out if the coin came up heads or tails. Forecasting the winter was hard enough, let alone what got everything going an eternity of winters ago.

Only, is it really true that there is no way of figuring it out? After all, the London churchman had been going to church his whole life. Presumably, he had reasons for believing the things he believed, just like any of us do. The reasons he had are just the ordinary reasons one has for one's religious beliefs, internal to the churchman's own religious views and practices. The problem, perhaps, was that envisioning himself being born in China made him want something more than those ordinary reasons. It made him want some reasons that could justify his current beliefs *independently from his current point of view*. It would be great if that aspiration could be realized. It would not only reassure him that he had justified beliefs. It would also empower him to demonstrate to anyone—whatever their current viewpoint might be—that his beliefs were the right ones. And what a power that would be!

However desirable, this dream might be impossible to achieve in real life.[4] The London churchman believes he's right about religion. He's just unnerved by the thought that he equally would have thought he was right about religion if he had been the Buddhist in China. But as the philosopher Roger White points out, we can always imagine being in a situation where we believed the opposite of what we now believe. That just goes with the territory of being the sort of creature who believes things. As White explains it: "Whenever we consider our most fundamental methods or epistemic standards we can feel that they require some kind of endorsement from the *outside*. But we run out of places to stand. We can't step outside of all reasoning, as it were, to assess whether any of our reasoning is any good. It is very hard to avoid a very general skepticism without having to admit that we can sometimes endorse our reasoning *from within*."[5]

This might sound like cold comfort. Don't worry, London churchman, because your fears about your religion apply to every single other belief you have!

How can this be good news? I'll adapt another case from White to try to get at why. Suppose I have no appreciation what-

4. As philosophers like to say, "Truth does not entail dialectical efficacy." (I think some of the snappiness of this line might be lost in translation. But, in a way, that's the point.) See Tristram McPherson and David Plunkett, "Deliberative Indispensability and Epistemic Justification," in *Oxford Studies in Metaethics*, vol. 10, ed. Russ Shafer-Landau (Oxford: Oxford University Press, 2015), 104–33.

5. Roger White, "You Just Believe That Because . . . ," *Philosophical Perspectives* 24 (2010): 573–615.

soever for museums. Museums, it seems to me, are like voluntarily doing homework for a class you didn't sign up for. But when I moved East, many of my friends liked going to museums. Let's suppose, hypothetically, that I should decide to impress my friends with my high-brow acumen. With daydreams of new-found urbanity, I start going to the museum. I walk around and look at the exhibits and linger over the informative placards and nod solemnly at docents' explanations. Somewhere along the way, let's suppose, I actually start to appreciate the history and art that museums offer. Going to the museum puts me in touch with—let's just suppose—some real reasons about what is valuable in the world. And so, newly acquainted with those reasons, I revise my beliefs in ways that actually become more sophisticated and appreciative of culture.

Now, imagine reformulating the skeptic's worry. "Your beliefs were caused by an arbitrary influence!" the skeptic says. And that is true. My desire to impress my friends had nothing at all to do with the truth. And it's also true that as a causal matter, I never would have formed any of my new beliefs except that I wanted to impress my friends. So, it seems that my new beliefs are formed under the influence of causes that are irrelevant to the truth.

Be that as it may, it shouldn't shake my confidence. Whatever you might say about my original plan, the truth is that my actions did in fact put me in touch with reasons that supported some beliefs about history, art, aesthetic value, and the like. So, there is nothing especially mysterious with updating my beliefs according to those reasons.

I admit this is all a bit hypothetical. For one thing, I never quite convinced my grad-school friends that I was a fancy person, and I hated going to the museum every single time. But never mind all that. Notice, we now have some resources to defend the London churchman. True, he came by his religious beliefs by way of his birthplace, a "mere accident" irrelevant to the truth of his religious views. But the arbitrariness of the origin of his views doesn't mean that he hasn't been in touch with real reasons for them, reasons which do bear on their truth. So, there is nothing amiss about forming his beliefs according to those reasons.

6

Are we looking up the canyon or down the canyon? My own youthful self thought both points of view were faulty. I had wanted there to be some point of view hovering, as it were, above the canyon and the valley both. From that lofty vantage point, an observer could see what was going on in a way that was independent from any arbitrary influence. Maybe that was a mistake. Maybe there was nothing like that. Maybe McCallister looks up the canyon because that's the way he can look from where he is right now. And maybe his wisdom is that he's come to terms with that being enough.

As he handed me the talk he had given in church twenty years before, Dad asked me what I wanted with it. "I've changed my mind recently about the moral of the story," I told him.

"What's the moral of the story?" he asked.

"Well, I used to think it was a mistake to look down the valley at the hides *and* a mistake to look up the valley at the haystacks," I said. "But now I think the moral is that looking up the valley was OK."

Dad pursed his lips slightly, dissatisfied. "I think the point is that they were both wise," he said.

"How's that?" I asked.

"Because they trusted each other," he said. I looked down at the talk, now in my hand. I had forgotten the title. "To Be Trusted Is Better Than to Be Loved," it read.

Conclusion

"Or what woman having ten silver coins, if she loses
one of them, does not light a lamp, sweep the house,
and search carefully until she finds it? When she has
found it, she calls together her friends and neighbors,
saying, 'Rejoice with me, for I have found the coin
that I had lost.'"

—Luke 15:8-9

Imagine the woman in Luke's parable before she lost her coin.
My guess is that the coins were no special source of happiness
for her. Of course, she'd be glad that she had them, but ten silver coins wouldn't be anything to celebrate over. Suppose she
had started with nine coins instead of ten. Would her happiness
have been much different? My guess is no. She would've felt
more or less the same.

But then she loses one coin, and she does absolutely everything to get it back. Finally, she finds it. When she does, she can't
contain her joy. Rejoicing in private is not enough. To express
her feelings, she must find others—her friends and neighbors—
to rejoice with her. She brings them together for a party. She
tells them not just how she feels but how she wants them to

feel.[1] "Rejoice with me," she says. She needs them to feel her joy as a kind of condition for living it herself. She doesn't have anything she didn't have at the start. It's still ten coins. She has only what she began with, but her perspective on it has changed. Jesus thinks the woman in the story is like us. And she is. Psychologists have run the parable again—except with chocolate rather than coins. If you eat a piece of chocolate alone in a room, you'll probably like it. But if you eat a piece of chocolate and some other person can see you eating that chocolate, then your experience of eating it is more vivid, specific, and memorable.[2] It doesn't matter if they're a stranger. It doesn't matter if you don't say a word to each other. They are there, with you.

In Mormon Zion, no one eats chocolate alone. Jesus compared the kingdom of God to the lost coin. Jesus's kingdom was not of this world; entering it didn't give you some material thing you didn't have before. It changed your perspective on what was already there.

Zion, I've suggested—or Mormon Zion anyway—is a kind of base camp for God's kingdom. In Mormon Zion, your perspective hasn't completely changed, wholesale, to accept a new reality. But neither do you have exactly the perspective with which you began. In that middle space, it's sometimes possible not only to catch a glimpse of another person's mind or heart but to share in what they're thinking or feeling—to be of one heart and one mind with them.

I understand that nothing I've said in the essays here will persuade you about anything. Forget persuasion. I want to leave you with one question and one personal aside.

1. See Amy-Jill Levine, *Short Stories by Jesus: The Enigmatic Parables of a Controversial Rabbi*, annotated ed. (San Francisco: HarperOne, 2015).

2. Erica J. Boothby, Margaret S. Clark, and John A. Bargh, "Shared Experiences Are Amplified," *Psychological Science* 25, no. 12 (December 2014): 2209-16, https://tinyurl.com/52ntuv7h.

The question: What three best moments do you most vividly remember from the last year? I'll give you mine. First, though, I want to be very clear about the rules. Rule #1: We're talking about good moments, not bad ones. Rule #2: They must be moments you really do remember—as in, you have a memory of them in your mind. These are not the moments that it seems like you *should* remember. Rule #3: They must be moments. You can't say, "visiting home at Christmas" or "that time we were on a road trip to Sacramento." Pick an actual moment, not a vague expanse of time.

OK, here are mine. (1) On a small lake in North Dakota, I caught a 27-inch walleye, and Andy—my sister's brother-in-law—gave me a high five. (2) I gave an academic talk at the University of Richmond, and afterward my best friend told me she was impressed. (3) At a university event, I debated a student about whether Snape was redeemed or not at the end of *Harry Potter*. Julia was funnier than I was, and I think if we had held a vote she would have won, but afterward she described it as a victory we had shared in together.

I don't know what's to be learned from your top three, but here is one takeaway from mine: if, somehow or other, the universe deals you a chance to respond to someone in a way that affirms, understands, or even shares in the way they value themselves, then you are in a position to give them a very special gift.

Here is the last thing: if you've read this far, thank you! In these essays, I've taken the liberty of leaving behind the style of academic philosophy. That you've taken time from your precious, one life to read this is a great gift to me. And if you haven't read this but just skipped to the last page to see what was here, that makes complete sense to me as well. Welcome to the last paragraph! Either way, I hope someday our paths cross again in a grocery store line or on a river or at an ice cream shop. See you in Zion!

Works Cited

Bailey, Olivia. "Empathy and the Value of Humane Understanding." *Philosophy and Phenomenological Research* 104, no. 1 (2022): 50–65. https://tinyurl.com/3cxyfrfz.

Barrett, Lisa Feldman. *How Emotions Are Made: The Secret Life of the Brain*. Boston: Mariner Books, 2017.

Bennett, Karen. *Making Things Up*. Oxford: Oxford University Press, 2017.

Bloom, Harold. *The American Religion*. New York: Chu Hartley Publishers, 2006.

Boothby, Erica J., Margaret S. Clark, and John A. Bargh. "Shared Experiences Are Amplified." *Psychological Science* 25, no. 12 (December 2014): 2209–16. https://tinyurl.com/52ntuv7h.

Bradley, Don. "'The Grand Fundamental Principles of Mormonism': Joseph Smith's Unfinished Reformation." *Sunstone*, April 2006, 32–41.

Brown, Samuel Morris. *Joseph Smith's Translation: The Words and Worlds of Early Mormonism*. New York: Oxford University Press, 2020.

Burton, Richard. *City of the Saints: Among the Mormons and Across the Rocky Mountains to California*, ed. Fawn M. Brodie. New York: Knopf, 1963.

Callard, Agnes. *Aspiration: The Agency of Becoming*. New York: Oxford University Press, 2018.

Works Cited

Church News. "Zion: LDS Roots Are Part of Park History," May 16, 1992. https://tinyurl.com/mt4hwuse.

Coons, Christian, and Michael Weber, eds. *Manipulation: Theory and Practice*. Oxford: Oxford University Press, 2014.

Crossan, John Dominic. *God and Empire: Jesus against Rome, Then and Now*. San Francisco: HarperOne, 2007.

———. *How to Read the Bible and Still Be a Christian: Is God Violent? An Exploration from Genesis to Revelation*. San Francisco: HarperOne, 2016.

———. *The Power of Parable: How Fiction by Jesus Became Fiction about Jesus*. San Francisco: HarperOne, 2013.

Darwall, Stephen. *The Second-Person Standpoint: Morality, Respect, and Accountability*. Cambridge, MA: Harvard University Press, 2006.

Davis, Ryan W. "Frontier Kantianism: Autonomy and Authority in Ralph Waldo Emerson and Joseph Smith." *Journal of Religious Ethics* 46, no. 2 (2018): 332–59. https://tinyurl.com/2s4j4v7w.

Dougherty, Matthew W. *Lost Tribes Found: Israelite Indians and Religious Nationalism in Early America*. Norman: University of Oklahoma Press, 2021.

Dover, Daniela. "Identity and Influence." *Synthese* 202, no. 5 (2023): 167. https://tinyurl.com/mveux9pa.

Emerson, Ralph Waldo. *Ralph Waldo Emerson: Essays and Lectures*. Library of America 15. New York: Literary Classics of the United States, 1983.

Givens, Terryl, and Nathaniel Givens. *Into the Headwinds: Why Belief Has Always Been Hard—and Still Is*. Grand Rapids: Eerdmans, 2022.

Godfrey, Kenneth W. "Charles W. Penrose: The English Mission Years." *Brigham Young University Studies* 27, no. 1 (1987): 113–26.

Hick, John. "Response to Hasker." In *Evidence and Religious Belief,* edited by Kelly James Clark and Raymond J. VanArragon, 199–201. Oxford: Oxford University Press, 2011.

Hobbes, Thomas. *Leviathan, with Selected Variants from the Latin Edition of 1668*. Edited by Edwin Curley. Indianapolis: Hackett, 1994.

Howard-Snyder, Daniel. "Who or What Is God, according to John Hick?" *Topoi* 36, no. 4 (December 2017): 571–86. https://tiny url.com/2catxrpz.

Inouye, Charles Shiro. *The End of the World, Plan B: A Guide for the Future*. Salt Lake City, UT: Greg Kofford Books, 2016.

Kaminsky, Joel, and Anne Stewart. "God of All the World: Universalism and Developing Monotheism in Isaiah 40–66." *Harvard Theological Review* 99, no. 2 (April 2006): 139–63. https:// tinyurl.com/3u9ea3c4.

Kant, Immanuel. *Kant: Groundwork of the Metaphysics of Morals*. 1785. Reprinted with translation by Mary Gregor and Jens Timmermann. 2nd ed. Cambridge: Cambridge University Press, 2012.

Korsgaard, Christine M. "Realism and Constructivism in Twentieth-Century Moral Philosophy." In "Philosophy in America at the Turn of the Century," edited by Robert Audi. Supplement, *Journal of Philosophical Research* 28 (October 2003): 99–122. https://tinyurl.com/33mmxvcf.

———. *Self-Constitution: Agency, Identity, and Integrity*. Oxford: Oxford University Press, 2009.

Kotkin, Joel. *Tribes: How Race, Religion and Identity Determine Success in the New Global Economy*. New York: Random House, 1993.

Lear, Jonathan. *Radical Hope: Ethics in the Face of Cultural Devastation*. Cambridge, MA: Harvard University Press, 2008.

Levine, Amy-Jill. *Short Stories by Jesus: The Enigmatic Parables of a Controversial Rabbi*. Annotated ed. San Francisco: HarperOne, 2015.

Levine, Amy-Jill, and Marc Zvi Brettler, eds. *The Jewish Annotated*

New Testament. 2nd ed. Oxford: Oxford University Press, 2017.

Machery, Edouard, Stephen Stich, David Rose, Amita Chatterjee, Kaori Karasawa, Noel Struchiner, Smita Sirker, Naoki Usui, and Takaaki Hashimoto. "Gettier across Cultures." *Noûs* 51, no. 3 (2017): 645–64. https://tinyurl.com/2ta5wp7f.

Mauss, Armand. *The Angel and the Beehive: The Mormon Struggle with Assimilation*. Urbana: University of Illinois Press, 1994.

———. "Sociological Perspectives on the Mormon Subculture." *Annual Review of Sociology* 10 (1984): 437–60.

May, Dean L. "Mormons." In *Harvard Encyclopedia of American Ethnic Groups*, ed. Stephan Thernstrom, Ann Orlov, and Oscar Handlin. Cambridge, MA: Harvard University Press, 1980.

McPherson, Tristram, and David Plunkett. "Deliberative Indispensability and Epistemic Justification." In *Oxford Studies in Metaethics*, vol. 10, edited by Russ Shafer-Landau, 104–33. Oxford: Oxford University Press, 2015.

Mill, John Stuart. *On Liberty, Utilitarianism and Other Essays*. Edited by Mark Philp and Frederick Rosen. 2nd ed. Oxford: Oxford University Press, 2015.

Moller, Dan. "Anticipated Emotions and Emotional Valence." *Philosopher's Imprint* 11, no. 9 (July 2011): 1–16. https://tinyurl.com/hjyh6nyv.

———. "The Boring." *The Journal of Aesthetics and Art Criticism* 72, no. 2 (2014): 181–91. https://tinyurl.com/yh3vjkbu.

Nagel, Thomas. *Mortal Questions*. Cambridge: Cambridge University Press, 1979.

Newbigin, Lesslie. *The Gospel in a Pluralist Society*. Grand Rapids: Eerdmans, 1989.

O'Dea, Thomas. "Mormonism and the Avoidance of Sectarian Stagnation: A Study of Church, Sect, and Incipient Nationality." *American Journal of Sociology* 60, no. 3 (November 1954): 285–93.

O'Neill, Onora. "Between Consenting Adults." *Philosophy & Public Affairs* 14, no. 3 (1985): 252–77.

Orsi, Robert A. *History and Presence.* 2016. Reprint, Cambridge, MA: The Belknap Press of Harvard University Press, 2018.

Penrose, Charles W. "Divisions of Modern Christendom—Effects of Sectarian Proselytism, Etc." Discourse presented at the Tabernacle, Salt Lake City, Utah, July 17, 1881. *Journal of Discourses Online* (blog). Joseph Smith Foundation. Accessed March 21, 2023. https://tinyurl.com/4ar4f8ym.

Phillips, D. Z. "Bad Faith and Sartre's Waiter." *Philosophy* 56, no. 215 (January 1981): 23–31.

Ritter, Josh. *Sermon on the Rocks.* Pytheas Recordings, 2015.

Rosen, Gideon. "Objectivity and Modern Idealism: What Is the Question?" In *Philosophy in Mind: The Place of Philosophy in the Study of Mind,* edited by Michaelis Michael and John O'Leary-Hawthorne, 277–319. Philosophical Studies Series. Dordrecht: Springer Netherlands, 1994.

Rowling, J. K. *Harry Potter and the Deathly Hallows.* London: Arthur A. Levine Books, 2017.

Sartre, Jean-Paul, *Being and Nothingness.* Translated by Hazel E. Barnes. London: Methuen and Co., 1969.

Scheffler, Samuel. *Equality and Tradition: Questions of Value in Moral and Political Theory.* Oxford: Oxford University Press, 2012.

Schmid, Konrad, and Jens Schröter. *The Making of the Bible: From the First Fragments to Sacred Scripture.* Translated by Peter Lewis. Cambridge, MA: The Belknap Press of Harvard University Press, 2021.

Setiya, Kieran. "Love and the Value of a Life." *The Philosophical Review* 123, no. 3 (July 2014): 251–80. https://tinyurl.com/pmz5 bup5.

Shalev, Eran. *American Zion: The Old Testament as a Political Text from the Revolution to the Civil War.* New Haven, CT: Yale University Press, 2014.

Smith, Joseph. Papers. Discourse, April 8, 1843, as reported by William Clayton-B. Church History Library, Salt Lake City, UT. https://tinyurl.com/y5z45jks.

———. Papers. Discourse, July 9, 1843, as reported by Willard Richards. Church History Library, Salt Lake City, UT. https://tinyurl.com/vxz5uyah.

———. Papers. Discourse, October 15, 1843, as reported by Willard Richards. Church History Library, Salt Lake City, UT. https://tinyurl.com/4yp395hz.

———. Papers. History, circa June 1839–circa 1841 [draft 2]. Church History Library, Salt Lake City, UT. https://tinyurl.com /3h7dn2fk.

———. Papers. History, circa summer 1832. Church History Library, Salt Lake City, UT. https://tinyurl.com/4eudkkcz.

———. Papers. Journal, 1835–1836. Church History Library, Salt Lake City, UT. https://tinyurl.com/mr246x8z.

———. Papers. Journal, December 1842–June 1844; Book 3, July 15, 1843–February 29, 1844. Church History Library, Salt Lake City, UT. https://tinyurl.com/ywcpm4as.

Swift, Taylor. *1989 (Taylor's Version)*. Republic Records, 2023.

———. *Fearless (Taylor's Version)*. Republic Records, 2021.

———. *Red (Taylor's Version)*. Republic Records, 2021.

———. *Speak Now*. Big Machine Records, 2010.

———. *Speak Now (Taylor's Version)*. Republic Records, 2023.

———. *Taylor Swift*. Big Machine Records, 2006.

Taves, Ann. *Revelatory Events: Three Case Studies of the Emergence of New Spiritual Paths*. Princeton: Princeton University Press, 2016.

Thatamanil, John J. *Circling the Elephant: A Comparative Theology of Religious Diversity*. New York: Fordham University Press, 2020.

Velleman, J. David. *Foundations for Moral Relativism*. Milton Keynes: Open Book Publishers, 2013.

———. "Identification and Identity." In *Self to Self: Selected Essays*, 2nd ed., 437–74. Ann Arbor: Michigan Publishing Services, 2020.

———. "Love as a Moral Emotion." In *Self to Self: Selected Essays*, 2nd ed., 86–136. Ann Arbor: Michigan Publishing Services, 2020.

———. "Self to Self." In *Self to Self: Selected Essays*, 2nd ed., 213–51. Ann Arbor: Michigan Publishing Services, 2020.

Wallace, R. Jay. *The View from Here: On Affirmation, Attachment, and the Limits of Regret*. Oxford: Oxford University Press, 2013.

White, Roger. "You Just Believe That Because . . ." *Philosophical Perspectives* 24 (2010): 573–615.

Wilson, Larry Y. "Take the Holy Spirit as Your Guide." Talk presented at the general conference of the Church of Jesus Christ of Latter-day Saints, Salt Lake City, Utah, April 1, 2018. Accessed March 13, 2023. https://tinyurl.com/t2p7f8t3.

Wright, Crispin. *Truth and Objectivity*. Cambridge, MA: Harvard University Press, 1993.

Wright, N. T. *Jesus and the Victory of God*. Vol. 2 of *Christian Origins and the Question of God*. Minneapolis: Fortress, 1997.

Wright, Robert. *The Evolution of God*. New York: Back Bay Books, 2010.

Yao, Vida. "Grace and Alienation." *Philosopher's Imprint* 20, no. 16 (2020): 1–18. https://tinyurl.com/ymxtamz4.